**NEW NELSON HISTORY** Townle

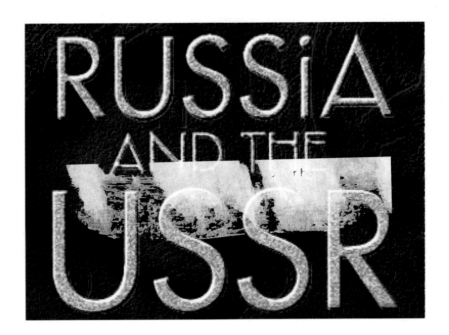

RUSSIA AND THE USSR

JOHN FOXON

Nelson

Acquisitions: Roda Morrison
Administration: Eileen Regan
Editorial: Catherine Dakin
Marketing: Jeremy Warner
Production:Ros Moon
Staff design: Lorraine Inglis
Typesetting: Fiona Webb

Thomas Nelson & Sons Ltd
Nelson House Mayfield Road
Walton-on-Thames Surrey
KT12 5PL UK

Thomas Nelson Australia
102 Dodds Street
South Melbourne
Victoria 3205 Australia

Nelson Canada
1120 Birchmont Road
Scarborough Ontario
M1K 5G4 Canada

© John Foxon 1997

First published by
Thomas Nelson and Sons Ltd 1997

ιⓉⲢ®   Thomas Nelson is an
International Thomson Publishing Company

ιⓉⲢ®   is used under licence

ISBN 0-17-4351089
NPN 9 8 7 6 5 4 3 2 1

Acknowledgements
The publishers are grateful to the following for permission to reproduce
copyright material:

Edimedia pp. 6 (left), 26
Gamma pp. 7 (centre left)
Hulton Deutsch pp. 7 (top right), 11 (top right), 17 (top two), 20 (bottom), 36-
39, 41, 63
Image Select pp. 6 (bottom left), 11 (top left), 22 (centre), 25, 30, 31, 52
David King pp. 22 (top and bottom),31, 32, 52, 55, 56, 57
Peter Newark's Military Pictures pp. 10 (bottom)
Novosti pp. 6 (top), 7 (top left), 8 (top), 13, 14, 18, 19 (left), 24, 30 (top), 32,
49, 62
Popperfoto pp. 7 (centre right), 11 (bottom left), 19 (right), 48, 61, 63
Society for the Cooperation in Russian and Soviet Studies pp. 4 (right),
7 (bottom), 42, 44, 45

Printed in Croatia

Contents

1 Overview

These two pictures convey vastly different images, although remarkably, only 60 years separates them. The people in these pictures look worlds apart, but they are of the same nationality – Russian.

In the twentieth century, enormous upheaval has taken place in this part of the world. There has been a change from the Tsarist Russian Empire to the Communist Union of Soviet Socialist Republics and, in the 1990s, to a Commonwealth of Independent States. Despite these changes, the peasants and the cosmonaut would have recognised the oppressive and autocratic methods of each other's society.

The key questions these photographs raise are: why did the old Russian Empire collapse and how did the new order of the Soviet Union develop?

Russian peasants in 1914.

Valentina Tereshkova, the world's first woman cosmonaut in 1963.

ASSIGNMENT

Imagine that the picture of the peasants and the picture of the cosmonaut are the first and last in an album of someone who has lived through all these changes. On the following page there are more pictures portraying people and events that span the twentieth century. Each photograph has a date and a page reference for where you can find it elsewhere in the book.

Use the photographs to build up an account of these changes and developments. Do this in the form of a timeline of the key events with brief descriptions. You could also produce brief profiles of some of the central personalities of these events – Tsar Nicholas II, Kerensky, Lenin, Trotsky, Stalin and Khrushchev.

1905 (page 6)

1905 (page 7)

1914 (page 17)

1917 (page 6)

1917 (page 6)

1917 (page 27)

1918 (page 31)

1919 (page 32)

1929 (page 37)

1929 (page 41)

1929 (page 44)

1930 (page 48)

(page 58)

1956 (page 63)

1956 (page 52)

2 The Causes of Unrest 1900–1914

The Russian revolutions

1905 Revolution Many Russian people were dissatisfied with the harsh and inefficient system of Russian government. In 1905, Russia went to war with Japan. The hope was that this would unite the people behind their Emperor, Tsar Nicholas II. The Russians, however, were soon defeated and the war caused food shortages, falling wages and unemployment.

A priest, Father Gapon, led a large procession of people to present a petition to the Tsar at the Winter Palace asking for his help. The Tsar was not there, but fearing trouble, the guards opened fire, killing many. This event became known as **Bloody Sunday**. It sparked off a series of strikes and rebellions throughout 1905, including a naval mutiny on the battleship *Potemkin*. To save himself, the Tsar agreed to have a parliament or **Duma** to advise him. After the 'revolution' was over however, he restated that *he* was in absolute control.

Revolution: March 1917 Russia went to war with Germany, on the side of Britain and France, in 1914. The ill-equipped, ill-fed and poorly led Russian army suffered defeat after defeat. At home, the Russian people were soon facing hardship and, by March 1917, there were severe food shortages. This led to riots in the capital, Petrograd, when the people demanded bread and an end to their suffering. Soldiers and police refused to fire on them. The Tsar was persuaded to abdicate (resign) and power passed to a committee known as the **Provisional Government**.

Revolution: November 1917 The Provisional Government did not last long. During 1917, revolutionaries, including the Bolshevik leader, Lenin (above left), arrived in Russia from exile. The Provisional Government was middle class and commanded little support from the working classes. The decision to carry on the war against Germany made them even more unpopular.

In November 1917, Lenin's Bolshevik Party seized power in an armed takeover of Petrograd and proclaimed that the Russian Empire was now a Communist state. All other political parties were soon abolished.

QUESTIONS

1 **How could you describe the political situation between 1905 and 1917?**

2 **Why were many Russians dissatisfied with the Tsar between 1905 and 1917?**

3 **How did the war with Japan and World War I help to cause the 1917 revolutions?**

4 **Were food shortages alone enough to cause the revolutions? Give reasons for your answer adding as many other causes of revolution as you can.**

Why did a revolutionary atmosphere develop in Tsarist Russia?

1

A large proportion of the wealth in Russia was owned by just a few people. Most Russians lived in conditions of poverty and endured lives of unrelieved hardship (see **Datapoint: Russian Society**). The conditions of the family shown here on the left were typical of many, including those who lived in towns. By contrast, life for the

Russian middle and upper classes was very comfortable. Pleasures such as this tea party (right) were quite commonplace for the well-to-do.

2

Russia was an autocracy. The Tsar had absolute power. The Russian Orthodox Church reinforced the idea that the Tsar had been chosen by God, and it was to God alone that the Tsar was responsible.
In 1900 an American, Henry Norman, wrote:

> *'Unless you realise that in Russia the Tsar is everything, his will is law, that his land and subjects are his to dispose of wholly at will... you will not grasp the condition of Russia today.'*

3

Russia lagged behind most other European countries in industrial and political development, but many Russians were beginning to learn about Western democracy and the advantages of industrialisation.

4

Karl Marx, a German writing in the mid-nineteenth century, described a 'communist' society where everyone was equal and the workers owned the means of production (e.g. factories and farms).
    Many educated Russians turned to political ideas emerging from other European countries. At first, they were attracted by the moderate ideas of democracy. However, as it increasingly became likely that the Tsar would resist even moderate changes, they were drawn towards socialism and in particular, the revolutionary ideas of Karl Marx, or **Marxism** (see **Datapoint: Political Ideas**).

Russian Society

1

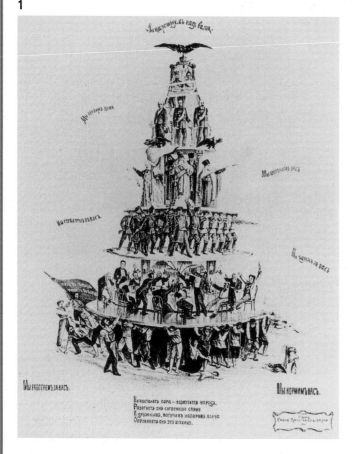

This picture was produced by Marxist Socialists as propaganda to show the workers why they should rise up against the Tsar and his wealthy supporters. It shows the divisions that existed in Russian society at that time. The workers are at the bottom supporting the Capitalists ('we do the eating'); above them are the army ('we do the shooting'); then the Russian Orthodox Church ('we mislead you'); and at the top, the royal family ('we rule you'). Because of press censorship in Russia, this picture was published in Switzerland.

2 Classes in Russian society 1900

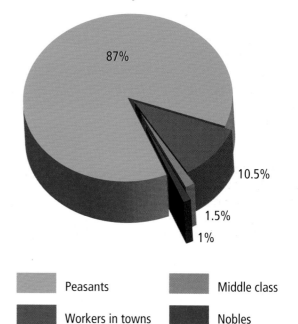

87%

10.5%

1.5%

1%

| ■ Peasants | ■ Middle class |
| ■ Workers in towns | ■ Nobles |

3

This peasants' hut looks temporary and ramshackle. It would have housed a large family and would have had no running water or sanitation.

The nobles controlled 50 per cent of the country's wealth. Their houses were grand and well-furnished. This picture shows one room of many in a large house.

How did revolutionary feeling develop into revolutionary action?

Revolutionary feeling did not suddenly develop at the start of the twentieth century. Revolutionary terrorists had been active during the latter half of the nineteenth century and had been successful in assassinating Tsar Alexander II in 1881. However, when Nicholas II became Tsar in 1894, it still appeared that the Tsarist government had a secure future. So what added fuel and sparks to the dry firewood of long-term dissatisfaction?

Imagine that sources 1 and 2 below are the firewood, 3 the fuel, 4 the match and 5 the fire bursting into flame.

1

Tsar Nicholas II believed in maintaining the autocracy of his ancestors, but he had little strength of character and not enough real interest in political affairs to make the right decisions to keep him in power. He applied oppressive methods, such as using the secret police to maintain his authority, and so lost the support of those he needed on his side. By making few concessions he had, in the end, to concede everything.

2

In 1905, the Tsar took bad advice from the Minister of the Interior, Plehve, and declared war on Japan. The idea was that the Russians would unite behind their Tsar in patriotic enthusiasm. Instead, the war caused more loss of faith in the Tsar and increased hardship for the Russian people. Part of the petition that Father Gapon hoped to present to the Tsar said:

'Lord, we workers, our children, our wives and our old, helpless parents have come, Lord, to seek truth and protection from you. We are impoverished and oppressed, unbearable work is imposed on us, we are despised and not recognised as human beings. We are treated as slaves who must bear the fate and be silent. We have suffered terrible things, but we are pressed ever deeper into the abyss of poverty, ignorance and lack of rights.'

3

Some of the middle and upper classes were becoming convinced that if Russia was to make progress, then the Tsar would have to share power with them at least. They tried to persuade him that if he did not, the lower classes would seize all the power for themselves.

4

The killing of the peaceful marchers in 1905 provoked a revolt in which the Tsar's uncle, the Governor General of St Petersburg, was assassinated. In June, the crew of the battleship *Potemkin* in the Black Sea port of Odessa mutinied, murdering officers on board. Although they gave themselves up a few weeks later, it was clear that the Tsar could no longer completely trust his armed forces. In September 1905, a general strike closed down factories, shops, railways, hospitals and schools. All over Russia, strikers set up workers' councils or **soviets.** They appeared to have more authority than the Tsar.

5

The Tsar was now under pressure to share some of his power. On 22 October 1905 Count Witte, a nobleman and former Minister of Finance warned the Tsar:

'The government must be ready to proceed along constitutional [democratic] lines.... There is no alternative. The government must either place itself at the head of the movement which has gripped the county or must relinquish it to the elementary forces to tear it to pieces.'

The Tsar accepted Witte's advice and issued a document called the **October Manifesto** which gave Russia its first elected parliament (Duma) to advise the Tsar on running the country. Russians were also allowed freedom of speech and the right to form political parties.

Political Ideas

The three main political parties at the beginning of the twentieth century were the **Constitutional Democrats**, the **Social Revolutionary Party** and the **Social Democratic Party**.

Constitutional Democrats	Social Revolutionaries	Social Democrats
ALSO KNOWN AS: Cadets	'SR's	Bolsheviks Mensheviks
IDEAS: • to persuade the Tsar to share his power • to have an elected parliament in a democratic system of government	• to abolish Tsarist rule • to redistribute land to the peasants	• to overthrow the existing order • to achieve a Marxist Socialist revolution
METHODS: • to peacefully criticise the government (to demand free speech)	• to incite peasants to rise against the Tsar • to use terrorism e.g. assassination	• to use a small, dedicated group to overthrow the Tsar in a swift two-stage revolution (Bolsheviks) • to work with the middle class to achieve democracy, and then have a working class revolution (Mensheviks)
MEMBERSHIP: • middle class liberals e.g. doctors, lawyers, teachers	• peasants led by students and intellectuals	• urban workers led by the educated lower middle classes

1

All history was about class struggles, for example, the landowners against the capitalists. The last struggle would be between the capitalists and the poorer classes (the peasants and workers).

Marxism

Karl Marx formed many of his ideas whilst working in the British Museum. He was supported by his fellow German, the Manchester factory owner, Friedrich Engels. Marx wrote many books and pamphlets, the foremost ones being *The Communist Manifesto* (1848) and *Das Kapital* (1867). His main ideas are outlined here.

2

This last struggle would be a violent revolution.

3

After the revolution, everyone would share the wealth and the workers would own the means of production (land, factories and banks). Marx called this stage **socialism**.

Peasants | Church
Capitalists
Landowners

4

Eventually the system would develop into a classless society with everyone paid according to their needs. This final stage, he called **communism**.

Russian Socialism

Many Russian intellectuals were inspired by Marx and joined the Social Democratic Party. There were, however, many differences of opinion within the party on how to achieve a revolution. George Plekhanov, one of the founders of the party, and his followers denounced the methods of revolutionaries who used bank robberies to fund their activities.

The followers of V. I. Lenin, the **Bolsheviks** (the majority group), wanted to run the revolution on their own terms and achieve communism rapidly. Jules Martov's minority group, the **Mensheviks** were prepared to work with others and wait longer for the workers to achieve final victory. In 1907 this split widened and the various groups co-operated little after that.

Not all Socialists were in the Social Democratic Party; one party, which had 107 seats in the first Duma, was called the Labour Group (in Russian: *Trudoviks*). Alexander Kerensky, a prominent figure in the March 1917 Revolution and future Prime Minister, was a leading Trudovik.

V.I.Lenin

Alexander Kerensky

George Plekhanov

Jules Martov

Q U E S T I O N S

1 Look at *Datapoint: Russian Society*. Why were the divisions in Russian society an important cause of unrest by 1905?

2 Why were Tsar Nicholas II's personal qualities such an important factor in Russian politics during the early years of the twentieth century?

3 Look at *Datapoint : Political Ideas*. What features do these parties have in common? Why were the Social Revolutionaries and Social Democrats a particular threat to the Tsarist government?

4 'The most important cause of revolutionary feeling by 1905 was Russia's backwardness.' Do you agree? Explain your answer fully.

Why was the Tsar able to survive up to 1917?

Despite the October Manifesto, it soon became clear that the Tsar intended that the Duma should have no real power. Out of the four dumas to meet between May 1906 and March 1917, only one lasted the full term; the others were dismissed by the Tsar for being too radical.

The middle classes were delighted with their involvement in politics, but the revolutionary parties were suspicious. Leon Trotsky, a leading revolutionary, felt that little had changed.

The revolutionaries had good cause to suspect the Tsar's motives. At the end of 1905, members of the St Petersburg Soviet were arrested and sent into exile whilst the army brutally crushed the Moscow Soviet, killing more than a thousand people.

By 1906, the revolution was over. As far as the Tsar was concerned nothing had changed – Russia was still an autocracy. The Tsar felt confident enough to reassert this by issuing the **Fundamental Laws**.

Isvestia

'We are a given a Witte but Trepov remains; we are given a constitution, but absolutism remains. All is given and nothing is given.'

The extract above was written by **Leon Trotsky** in the first copy of the revolutionary newspaper, *Isvestia*. The more liberal Witte had recently become Prime Minister. Trepov was at this time Governor of St Petersburg and was regarded as ruthless despite his welcoming of the reforms in the October Manifesto.

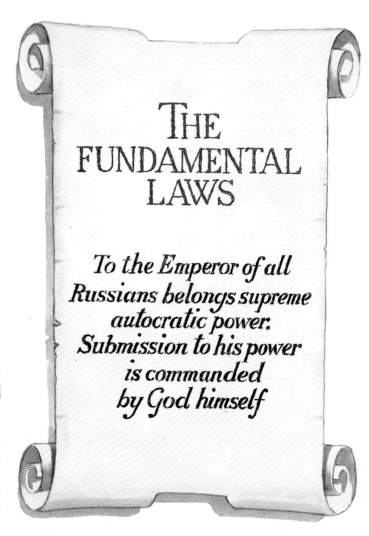

THE FUNDAMENTAL LAWS

To the Emperor of all Russians belongs supreme autocratic power. Submission to his power is commanded by God himself

Despite the challenge to his power Nicholas was, in fact, able to survive as Tsar until March 1917. What had enabled him to prolong his power? He was fortunate in having the general loyalty of the peasants and army and, although he himself had few political skills, he appointed a man who had the expertise to strengthen his regime, Peter Stolypin. Stolypin combined concessions with harshness.

Concession

Stolypin abolished the redemption payments that the peasants had been paying since they were freed from serfdom (slavery) in 1861. He encouraged the richer peasants (kulaks) to buy out the poorer peasants, thus creating larger, modern and more efficient farms, and a kulak class who would be loyal supporters of the Tsar.

The peasants remembered that Nicholas' grandfather, Alexander II, had freed them from serfdom. They were largely uneducated and easily influenced by the Russian Orthodox Church, which proclaimed the Tsar as God's representative on earth. To the Russian peasant, the Tsar was their 'Little Father'. It was the peasants who provided the large numbers for the army.

Peter Stolypin was the only man who had the political imagination to save the Tsar's government. After his death the Tsar was unable to find another strong minister.

Harshness

In 1906 Stolypin had 21,000 people exiled to Siberia and 1008 people executed. The hangman's noose became known as 'Stolypin's Neck-tie'. Stolypin crushed the 1905 Revolution for the Tsar and continued arresting opponents. He ensured that the police and the armed forces maintained their discipline and allegiance to the Tsar.

After 1906 conditions seemed to improve – industry expanded, wages increased, and harvests were good. Strikes decreased, and from 1908 to 1911, were virtually non-existent. At the same time, peasant risings also declined significantly.

The calm on the surface, however, disguised the trouble below. Stolypin encouraged the improvement of education but now the more literate peasants began to understand and resent the system which kept them in poverty. Many were angry at the rise of the kulak class. Then, in 1911, Stolypin was murdered by a Social Revolutionary. From 1912 strikes began to increase once more and the Duma, now largely made up of landowners and urban property owners, began to complain about the police and government policy. Pressure was beginning to mount against the Tsar once again.

In 1914 the Tsar took Russia into World War I, believing that war would rescue his ailing regime. Instead, it was to be his downfall!

QUESTIONS

1 **What contribution did Peter Stolypin make to the Tsar's survival in power after the 1905 Revolution?**

2 **Did the 1905 Revolution achieve the aims of those who wanted change?**

3 **The relative calm after 1915 was only on the surface. What evidence is there to support this view?**

4 **How well did the Tsar cope with the political situation in the years 1916–14?**

5 **'By 1914 the Tsar's chances of surviving for much longer were limited'. Is this statement accurate? Give a detailed answer looking at the different sides of the argument.**

The 1905 Revolution

'On this day [21 January] the priest Gapon prepared and distributed a petition from the workers addressed to the sovereign, in which rude demands of a political nature were expressed along with wishes for changes in working conditions. Gapon... excited the workers to such an extent that on 22nd January they began heading in great throngs toward the centre of the city. In some places, bloody clashes took place between workers and troops because of the stubborn refusal of the crowd to obey the command to go home, and sometimes even because of attacks on the troops...

The number of victims on 22nd January proved to be, by accurate count: 96 dead and 333 wounded.'

'Official Report of Events', 23 January 1905, published in the journal *Pravo* (Justice), No 2, 31 January 1905.

SOURCE A

'The people believe in Thee. They have made up their minds to gather at the Winter Palace tomorrow at 2 p.m. to lay their needs before Thee... Do not fear anything. Stand tomorrow before the party and accept our humblest petition. I, the representative of the working men, and my comrades, guarantee the inviolability of Thy person.'

Father Gapon, extract from a letter written to the Tsar on 21 January 1905, the day before Bloody Sunday.

SOURCE C

This picture by **O. G. Betekhtin**, was painted in 1955. Do the crowd seem as aggressive as described in Source B?

SOURCE D

'21st January 1905. A clear frosty day. There was much activity and many reports. Fredericks came to lunch. Went for a long walk. Since yesterday all the factories and workshops in St Petersburg have been on strike. Troops have been brought in to strengthen the garrison. The workers have conducted themselves calmly hitherto. At the head of the workers union is a Socialist priest: Gapon.

22nd January 1905. A painful day. There have been serious disorders in St Petersburg because workmen wanted to come up to the Winter Palace. Troops had to open fire in several places in the city; there were many killed and wounded. God, how painful and sad! Mama arrived from town, straight to church. I lunched with all the others. Went for a walk with Misha. Mama stayed overnight.'

Tsar Nicholas II, extracts from his diary.

SOURCE E

'...Suddenly the company of Cossacks galloped rapidly towards us with drawn swords. So, then, it was to be a massacre after all! There was no time for consideration, for making plans, or giving orders. A cry of alarm arose as the Cossacks came down upon us. Our front ranks broke before them, opening on to right and left, and down the lane the soldiers drove their horses, striking on both sides.... An old man named Lavretiev, who was carrying the Tsar's portrait, had been one of the first victims. Another old man caught the portrait

as it fell from his hands and carried it till he too was killed by the next volley. With his last gasp the old man said "I may die, but I will see the Tsar".... At last the firing ceased. I stood up with a few others who remained uninjured and looked down at the bodies that lay prostrate around me.... Horror crept into my heart. The thought flashed through my mind. "And this is the work of our Little Father, the Tsar."'

Father Gapon managed to escape. He wrote this account in *The Story of My Life* (1905).

QUESTIONS

1 **What does Source A tell you about the conditions of the ordinary Russian people?**

2 **Look at Sources C and E. What kind of force did the Cossacks use against the marchers?**

3 **Look at Sources A and E. How does Gapon describe the marchers' feelings towards the Tsar?**

4 **Sources B and E give different interpretations of the events of Bloody Sunday. How would you account for these differences?**

5 **How useful is Source D in showing the attitude of the Tsar towards his people? Explain your answer.**

6 **Source B was written by the Tsar's officials and Source C was painted in 1955 by a Communist artist. How do these facts affect their reliability? Explain your answer. If they are not fully reliable does this affect their usefulness? Explain your answer.**

7 **'The 1905 Revolution was caused by the Tsar's government over-reacting to the march on the Winter Palace.' Do you agree? Explain your answer fully using all the sources and you own knowledge.**

3 The Collapse of Tsarist Russia

The Tsar expected World War I (1914–18) to be a quick and resounding victory which would restore the people's faith in his regime. Instead, after a few early victories, the Russian army suffered defeat after defeat and the country lost faith in him. The Tsar had survived a revolution in 1905 but there had been signs of more trouble in the years leading up to 1914.

In March 1917, the situation had deteriorated so much that Tsar Nicholas felt it necessary to abdicate (resign) from his position. There was no one willing to take his place as Tsar and so Russia became a republic. The important question for historians is: why was the Tsar weakened by World War I?

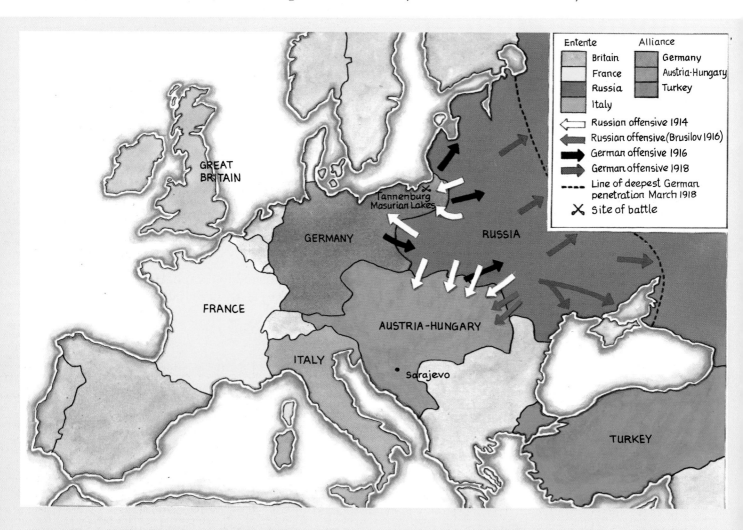

In 1914, a Serb murdered the heir to the Austrian Empire in Sarajevo, Bosnia. This incident led to World War I. Russia entered the war in August 1914 to protect fellow Slavs in Serbia from the aggression of Germany and Austria. At first the war was popular with most Russians. The Tsar thought that the great Russian army, combined with the British and French, was bound to win by Christmas. In fact the war lasted until 1918, by which time more than nine million Russian soldiers had been killed or wounded. The war was one of the decisive factors in the collapse of the Tsar's regime.

1

Despite its huge size the Russian army was out of date and inefficient compared both to its allies and its enemies. Successes were few and defeats were many. The poorly led peasant army suffered enormous casualties.

4

Rasputin (meaning 'disreputable one') was the name given to a Russian holy man who gained the trust of the Tsar and his family. He was a drunkard and a womaniser, but he claimed to have supernatural powers and seemed to be able to control the Tsar's son Alexis' life-threatening blood disease of haemophilia. The Tsar's wife, Alexandra was under his spell. Rasputin's hold over the family gained him considerable influence and he was open to bribes from those wanting ministerial posts or government contracts.

Rasputin was murdered in December 1916 by a group of nobles jealous of his influence and concerned that his scandalous behaviour would bring down the monarchy.

2

'*Within Russia, meanwhile, the war was straining a badly integrated economy, exposing the weak spots of agriculture, industry and the transportation system. On the already heavily taxed nation fell the added burden of war. Every day of fighting in 1915 required an expenditure of 25.7 million roubles; in 1916 this sum had jumped to 41.7 million roubles.... Agriculture and industry were badly hit by conscription. Eighteen million men, nearly half of the adult working population, were called up.... For the inefficient conduct of the war and the short-sighted approach to domestic affairs the responsibility fell squarely on the shoulders of Tsar Nicholas.*'
David Shub, *Lenin* (1948).

Shub was a member of the Social Democratic Party. He escaped to the USA after the 1905 Revolution but kept in touch with the revolutionary leaders.

5

In August 1915 the Tsar took over as Commander-in-Chief of the Russian army. This was a disastrous move for him for two reasons: firstly, he was a poor military leader and secondly, the Russians could now blame him personally for every defeat.

The Tsar is shown here blessing his troops while they kneel in respect.

3

The winter of 1916–17 was even more severe than usual. The shortages of fuel and food drove the people to even greater despair. In March 1917 bread shortages, particularly in Petrograd, led to strikes and riots. The once-loyal troops and police refused to fire on the crowds and turned on their officers instead. To try and salvage something for himself and Russia, the Tsar abdicated. Russia was now a republic run by a twelve-man committee of the Russian Duma (parliament).

Causes of Discontent in 1916–17

1 Russian casualties by 1917

Total forces:	12,000,000

Total casualties:	9,150,000

Total casualties as percentage of total mobilised: 76.3%

2 Army desertions

February 1917: 7,000

March 1917: 34,000

3 Food prices in roubles

	Meat	Potatoes	Bag of wheat flour
1913	0.48	1.0	2.5
1917	2.80	7.0	16.0

4 Number of strikes

August to December 1914: 50
January to February 1917: 1350

1914 **1917**

Diary of the March Revolution of 1917

'The new year 1917 began with blizzards and temperatures as low as 35 degrees below zero. More than a thousand railway engines froze and burst their boilers. Supplies of grain, coal, wood and oil dwindled to nothing.'

Josh Brooman, *Russia in War and Revolution (1986)*.

The winter, food shortages and dissatisfaction with the war hastened the downfall of the Tsar. When it came, it came swiftly.

7 March:
20,000 workers locked out of Putilov Steel Works in a pay dispute. Other workers go on strike in support.

8 March:
50 factories close down, 90,000 workers on strike. Thousands of Socialist women in Petrograd commemorate International Women's Day (see picture below).

'...a poor woman entered a bread shop...and asked for bread. She was told there was none. On leaving the shop, she saw bread in the window and took it. A General, passing in his motor, stopped and remonstrated with her. A crowd collected round them, smashed his motor and, increasing in size, paraded the streets asking for bread.'

Sybil Grey, an Englishwoman living in Petrograd, writing in her diary.

9 March:
Half of Petrograd now on strike.

'Throughout the entire day, crowds of people poured from one part of the city to another.... Around the barracks, sentinels, patrols and lines of soldiers, stood groups of working men and women exchanging friendly words with army men.'

Leon Trotsky, *History of the Russian Revolution (1933)*.

10 March:

250,000 workers on strike. Newspapers and transport brought to a halt. Cossacks refuse an order to attack a procession of strikers.

11 March:

The President of the Duma urges the Tsar to find someone who is supported by the people to form a new government. The Tsar orders the Duma to stop meeting.

> *'The situation is serious. The capital is in a state of anarchy; the government is paralysed; the transport system has broken down; the food and fuel supplies are completely disorganised. Discontent is general and on the increase.'*

Michael Rodsianko, the President of the Duma, in a telegram to the Tsar.

12 March:

A Sergeant shoots dead his Commanding Officer. Soldiers then leave their barracks to join the protesters in the city. The Duma continues to meet and sets up a twelve-man committee to take over the government. At the same time revolutionaries, soldiers and workers form a soviet (council), also with the aim of taking over government.

> *'Serious mutiny has broken out among the troops and all the men we saw belong to regiments sent to restore order, who, after firing a few volleys, made common cause with the mutineers.'*

Louis de Robien, French diplomat, living in Petrograd writing in his diary.

13 March:

The Tsar offers to share power with the Duma. **Michael Rodzianko** replies:

> *'The measures you propose are too late. The time for them has gone. There is no return.'*

14 March:

Army generals tell the Tsar that none of the army support him any more.

15 March:

The Tsar abdicates in favour, first, of his son Alexis, but as he is too ill the Tsar gives the crown to his brother Michael.

> *'The Emperor entered the hall. After bowing to everybody, he made a short speech. He said that the welfare of his country, the necessity for putting an end to the Revolution and preventing the horrors of civil war…had determined him to abdicate in favour of his brother, the Grand Duke Michael Alexandrovich.'*

General Lukomsky, assistant to the Chief-of-Staff.

Michael fears for his life and abdicates within 24 hours. Russia is now a republic but who controls the government – the Duma Committee or the Petrograd Soviet?

Painting of the Abdication of the Tsar.

Why did the Tsar abdicate in March 1917?

The immediate reason for the Tsar's abdication was that his generals could no longer guarantee him the support of the army.

This was not the only cause of his downfall, however, which had been a long time coming.

ASSIGNMENT

Look at the following factors leading to the Tsar's abdication. They have not been placed in order of importance, the numbers are for reference only. You should first group them under the headings **Underlying** (long-term), **Intermediate** (medium-term) and **Immediate** (short-term) causes of the abdication of the Tsar in March 1917. You should then place them in order of importance.

Finally, identify the causes over which Tsar Nicholas had some degree of control and those that were beyond his control.

1
On 14 March, generals informed the Tsar that none of the army supported him.

2
The winter of 1916–17 was exceptionally cold.

3
On 12 March 1917, police and soldiers joined the rioting crowds in Petrograd.

4
While the Tsar led the army, the government was left in the hands of his German wife, Tsarina Alexandra (right) who was influenced by Rasputin.

5
Opposition parties critical of the Tsar were growing. Many were talking of revolution. One such group, the Bolsheviks, were particularly determined to overthrow the Tsar. They were led by a man of iron will, Lenin, who kept them under strict discipline even while he was in exile in Switzerland.

6
The Russian army was badly organised, ill-equipped, badly fed and poorly led by the Tsar. Soldiers deserted in their thousands.

Two Russian deserters being attacked by a supporter of the Tsar.

7

Russia went to war with Germany and Austria in 1914.

8

The Tsar was an autocrat who wanted to keep his God-given power.

'The gentle but uneducated Emperor...is weak on every point except his own autocracy.'

Sir Arthur Nicholson, The British Ambassador to Russia in 1906.

9

Over 90 per cent of the population were workers or peasants, but they only owned about one per cent of the wealth.

10

Tsar Nicholas was a weak man who was easily influenced by officials.

'The daily work of a ruler he found terribly boring. He could not stand listening long or seriously to ministers' reports, or reading them. He liked such ministers as could tell an amusing story and did not weary his attention with too much business.'

Alexander Kerensky (1906). He became Prime Minister in the Provisional Government in 1917.

11

Nicholas did not understand the hardships faced by peasants and workers.

'His mentality and his circumstances kept him wholly out of touch with the people. He heard of the blood and tears of thousands upon thousands only through official documents.'

Alexander Kerensky (1906).

12

The Tsar's government mismanaged the economy and the Russians were short of essential supplies during the war.

13

Russia was backward compared to many other countries. Germany had a hundred times as many factories as Russia.

14

In March 1917, over half of Petrograd was on strike in protest over bread and fuel shortages.

Q U E S T I O N S

1   **Why was the Tsar weakened by World War I?**

2   **What responsibility did the Tsarina Alexandra and Rasputin have for the Tsar's downfall?**

3   **Why was losing the support of the armed forces such a disaster for the Tsar?**

4   **Which causes of his downfall were of the Tsar's own making?**

5   **'If the Tsar had not led his army into war the Russian Revolution of March 1917 would have been avoided.' Give a full explanation of whether you think this is an accurate view of the causes of the March Revolution.**

Why did the Provisional Government lose power to the Bolsheviks in November 1917?

After the Tsar's abdication, it was not clear who governed Russia. The rivals for power were the Petrograd Soviet (Council of Workers and Soldiers) and the Duma committee which now called itself the Provisional Government.

The Provisional Government planned to hold elections to create an Assembly which would decide upon a new constitution. These elections were scheduled for November 1917. By the time they were held, however, the Provisional Government had been toppled from power. How did this happen?

The Petrograd Soviet at a meeting of the State Duma, 1917.

The Petrograd Soviet was a council of workers and soldiers. At first the Soviet co-operated with the Provisional Government, but increasingly it issued its own orders. This was especially the case after Lenin's return from exile, when the Bolsheviks began to take over the soviets. There were soviets in all the major cities of Russia and they appeared to have far more authority than the Provisional Government.

Alexander Kerensky (left in the picture) was a brilliant speaker, even out-performing Lenin on one occasion. He came from a socialist background, but after he became Prime Minister for the Provisional Government, his socialism became less apparent and he seemed to adopt some of the attitudes of the Tsar's regime.

At first the excitement of power hid divisions between the various groups. As the problems grew the divisions widened, especially as the Bolsheviks refused to co-operate with the Provisional Government.

This picture shows a crowd in Petrograd scattering to avoid the bullets fired by troops loyal to the Provisional Government. The Bolsheviks had organised the rising in July 1917. Kerensky ordered his troops to put down the rising, which they did, killing and wounding 400 of the crowd.

Many historians believe that it was a series of mistakes by the Provisional Government which led to its downfall. Look at the following events and explain the effect of each one. Then analyse how their collective effect caused the Provisional Government to lose power.

EVENT	EFFECT
1 The Provisional Government introduced democratic measures such as releasing political prisoners, lifting controls on the press and trade unions, allowing the return of exiled revolutionaries and giving their opponents political freedoms.	
2 The Provisional Government opted to continue the war. In June the Russian army launched a major attack against Austria, which soon failed and turned into a retreat. As a result, the government lost the support of the army.	
3 The Provisional Government did not give the peasants the land they demanded.	
4 The Germans wanted the Russians out of the war so that they could concentrate on fighting the British and French. They helped Lenin to return to Russia from exile in Switzerland. Lenin ordered the Bolsheviks in the Petrograd Soviet not to co-operate with the government. He published his April Theses, in which he demanded: **peace**; **bread** for the workers; **land** for the peasants and **all power to be given to the soviets.**	
5 The Bolsheviks organised riots in July (the July Days). The Provisional Government crushed them but failed to capture Lenin.	
6 When faced with a right-wing revolt led by General Kornilov in August, Kerensky, now Prime Minister, turned to the Bolsheviks for support and gave them weapons to fight with. The Bolsheviks played a large part in defeating Kornilov and gained popularity. They also kept the weapons.	

The November Revolution

By autumn 1917, the Bolsheviks were in the majority in the Petrograd and Moscow Soviets. Lenin had always maintained that the revolution could only be successfully carried out by a small dedicated group. By October 1917, he was convinced that the time was coming for his Bolsheviks to take power and he ordered Leon Trotsky, as Chairman of the Military Revolutionary Committee, to draw up plans to take over the key points of the city.

1 The Bolshevik militia were known as the **Red Guards**. They were mainly factory workers, armed with rifles and other weapons acquired after the Kornilov Revolt.

On the night of 6 November the plan was put into operation. By the following morning the key positions were in the hands of the Bolsheviks.

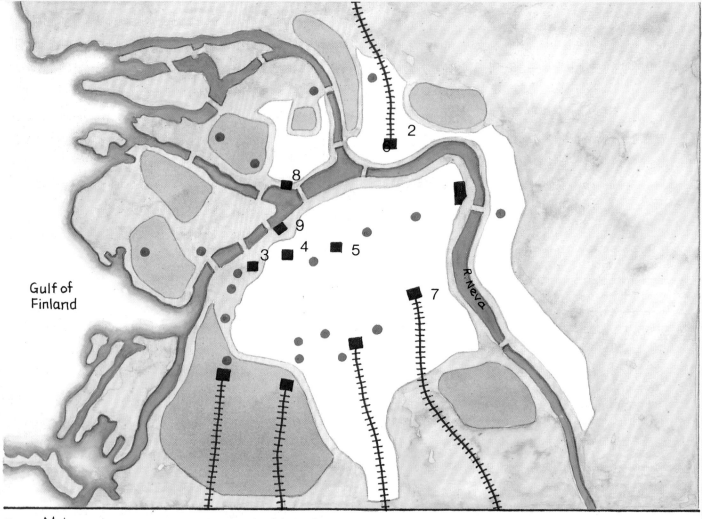

Gulf of Finland

R. Neva

● Main army barracks

▮ Industrial areas

1 Smolny Institute (a famous school which in November 1917 became the Bolshevik headquarters)
2 Vyborg District
3 Central Post Office
4 Telegraph Office
5 State Bank
6 Finland Station
7 Moscow Station
8 St Peter and St Paul Fortress (built in 1703 to protect the city)
9 Winter Palace (the Tsar's palace)

2

On the evening of 7 November, the captured cruiser *Aurora* fired blank shells at the Winter Palace, the headquarters of the Provisional Government. This signalled the beginning of the Bolshevik takeover.

3

During the night of the 6 and the morning of the 7 November, the Red Guards took command of all of the most important locations in Petrograd. They first took control of six bridges across the River Neva, and then seized government buildings, the power station and railway station. They were now in control of communications and could monitor all movements into, out of and across the city.

4

After the *Aurora* opened fire, Trotsky's Red Guards stormed the Winter Palace, overpowered the Cadets and the Women's Battalion defending it, and captured the Provisional Government (with the exception of Kerensky who had escaped). Eighteen people were arrested and two people killed.

By November 1917, the Provisional Government had lost the support of the army to the extent that only the Women's Battalion (above) and Cadet Officers (young trainees) were left to defend the Winter Palace.

5

By 8 November, the Bolsheviks were in control. Lenin issued posters proclaiming:

'To the citizens of Russia! The Provisional Government is overthrown. State power has passed into the hands of...the Military Revolutionary Committee which stands at the head of the Petrograd proletariat [workers] and garrison [soldiers].'

QUESTIONS

1 **Why was it important for the Bolsheviks to control transport and communications?**

2 **A 'revolution' usually involves a large number of people achieving dramatic change. A 'coup' involves a small group of people taking power, often for their own ends. Which of these do you think best describes the events of November 1917? Explain your answer carefully.**

3 **Explain which of these factors you think contributed most to the 'Bolshevik Revolution', the failure of the Provisional Government or the work of Lenin.**

A popular rising?

SOURCE C

'The citizen slept in peace ignorant of the change from one power to another.... Peter and Paul Fortress is today completely taken possession of.... Machine guns are set up on the fortress wall to command the quay and the bridge.'

Leon Trotsky, *History of the Russian Revolution* (ed. 1965). Trotsky was in charge of the Red Guards and was keen to stress the smoothness of the operation.

SOURCE A

'Like a black river, filling all the street, without song or cheer, we poured through the Red Arch.... In the open we began to run, stooping low and bunching together, and jammed up suddenly behind the Alexander Column.... After a few minutes huddling there, some hundreds of men, the Army seemed reassured and without any orders began again to flow forward.... On both sides of the main gateway the door stood wide open, light streamed out, and from the building came not a single sound.... The cadets came out in single bunches of three and four. The Communists seized upon them with remarks...but no violence was done.'

John Reed, *Ten Days That Shook the World* (1926). Reed was an American journalist and Communist living in Petrograd at the time. His book combines eyewitness accounts, what he was told, and what he thought was likely to happen. The arch, gateway and column referred to can be seen in Source E.

SOURCE D

'He [Lenin] frequently addressed mass rallies and meetings.... Lenin's speeches, noted for their profound content and brilliant delivery, inspired the workers and soldiers to a determined struggle.'

Y. Kukushkina, a Soviet historian, *History of the USSR* (1981).

SOURCE B

'On November 7th the Red Guard, composed mainly of factory workers, occupied key positions in the city and advanced on the Winter Palace. It was a bloodless coup. The Provisional Government collapsed without resistance.'

E. H. Carr, *The Russian Revolution From Lenin to Stalin* (1979).

SOURCE E

This painting *Storming of the Winter Palace* by Pavel Sokolov-Skalia, a Russian Communist, was produced in 1937 to show the achievement of the Bolshevik Revolution.

QUESTIONS

1   Which group captured the Provisional Government in the Winter Palace?

2   Source E gives a different impression of the capture of the Winter Palace to the other sources. How would you account for this?

3   What do you learn from Source A about the events of 7 November?

4   As Trotsky (Source C) was involved in these events does this make his evidence more reliable than that of E. H. Carr (Source B), who was not? Explain your answer carefully.

5   Kukushkina is a Soviet historian and, therefore, has a particular viewpoint. Explain in detail whether this means his evidence is of little use in understanding the events of November 1917.

6   Using all the sources, do you think it is more accurate to describe the events of November 1917 as a well-organised takeover by dedicated revolutionaries, or a popular rising of the workers against the Provisional Government? Give reasons for your answer.

4 The Formation of the USSR 1917–1924

How did the Bolsheviks consolidate their power?

Lenin and his Bolshevik Party had seized power in Petrograd, but what about the rest of the Russian Empire? Russia was an enormous country, covering one-sixth of the world's land surface. To take complete power of it would not be easy, and Lenin and his Bolshevik government faced many difficult problems for which they would need to quickly find solutions.

Problems

The Tsar was still alive. He was, to some, a symbol that the monarchy might return.

Russia's citizens had just got used to freedom and the idea of democracy. Would they accept the dictatorship of one man and one party?

Russia was still at war. It could be invaded by Germany or even, by its allies who were keen to keep Russia in the war.

Russia was incredibly backward. The more advanced parts of its economy, banks, industry and transport, were in the hands of rich, private individuals.

Most of Russia was agricultural. Lenin needed support from the peasants who at present favoured the Social Revolutionaries.

The Bolsheviks were just one of the many groups who wanted to take over Russia. Some of the other groups appeared to be more popular and might win greater support in the forthcoming elections to the Constituent Assembly.

Decrees of Sovnarkom, 1917

These were some of the government decrees following the Revolution.

8 November: 540 million acres of land was taken away from the Tsar, the nobles and the Church and given to the peasants to divide amongst themselves.

12 November: A decree on work established an eight-hour day and forty-eight hour week for all industrial workers and set rules for holidays and overtime.

1 December: A decree on the Press banned all non-Bolshevik newspapers.

11 December: The Constitutional Democratic Party was banned and its leaders arrested.

20 December: The political police force, the Cheka, was set up to deal with opponents of the Bolsheviks.

27 December: Banks were put in the control of the government and factories were put under the control of elected committees of workers.

Solutions

Lenin formed a government of fifteen Bolsheviks, known as the COUNCIL OF PEOPLES COMMISSARS (Sovnarkom), with himself as chairman. The capital was moved to Moscow, further inland and safe from foreign invasion.

The peasants were allowed to seize their landlords' land.

The elections to the Constituent Assembly were allowed to continue, but as less than half of the elected members were Bolsheviks the Red Guards closed it after one day.

The war with Germany was ended in March 1918 by the signing of the Treaty of Brest-Litovsk. Russia's agony was over but she lost valuable resources in the Treaty.

Only Communist (Bolshevik) newspapers were allowed. The CHEKA (secret police) was created. In 1918 it executed 50,000 of the Bolshevik's opponents.

The Government took control of banks, industry and transport, and confiscated the land and wealth of the Russian Orthodox Church.

Although Lenin had begun to address the early problems of consolidating power, they were not yet completely solved. Despite the secret police, there were still many opponents of Bolshevism. When World War I ended in November 1918, Russia's former allies began to combine with the Bolshevik's opponents to try and overthrow them. This led to civil war. The future of Bolshevik Russia was still in the balance.

Why did the Bolsheviks win the civil war?

The Whites

This Bolshevik cartoon shows Generals Denikin and Yudenich, and Admiral Kolchak, leaders of the armed opposition to the Bolsheviks. The fourth figure represents the United States of America. The cartoon is trying to convince its audience that the opposition are controlled by foreigners, like dogs on a lead. 'Whites' was the name given to the enemies of the Bolsheviks (the 'Reds'). On the side of the Whites were all who opposed the Bolsheviks. They were supported by foreign armies sent by Russia's former allies and by former Russian-held Czech prisoners of war, the Czech Legion. They had little unity or solidarity and never came together as a fighting force. Their successes, greater in the beginning, became few and far between. As the war progressed, the Bolsheviks were able to pick off each White group one by one. By the end of 1919 only isolated groups of Whites were fighting.

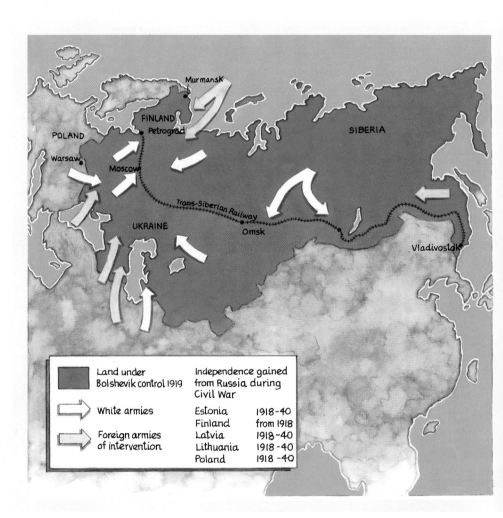

Map showing key actions of the civil war

The Red Terror

In August 1918 Lenin was seriously wounded when he was shot by a Socialist Revolutionary, Fanya Kaplan. The shooting convinced Lenin that more ruthless methods were needed to deal with opponents. Felix Dzerzhinsky, head of the Cheka, began the 'Red Terror'. Cheka units roamed the countryside and beat, hanged, shot and burned anyone suspected of helping or fighting for the Whites. The Cheka was even feared by loyal Bolsheviks.

Death of the Tsar

The Tsar is shown here in 1918 surrounded by his Bolshevik guards. The Tsar and his family had been prisoners of the Bolsheviks since the November Revolution and in 1918, they were being held away from the capital at Ekaterinburg in the Ural Mountains. In July 1918 it looked as if the Czech Legion were about to capture the town and release the Tsar. If that were to happen the Tsar would be free to lead the White armies, which would boost their morale.

The Bolsheviks realised that while the Tsar was alive, he could be a symbol of hope to their opponents. Rather than risk this, they shot dead the Tsar and his family and destroyed their bodies. There was now no rallying point for the Whites.

Leon Trotsky and the Red Army

At the start of the war, the Bolsheviks introduced compulsory military service (conscription) for all men aged eighteen to forty. This new army, the **Red Army**, was organised by Trotsky. He needed experienced officers, so he gave the skilled former officers of the Tsar two choices: either join the Red Army, or be sent to a prison camp. Any officer who tried to desert would find his family taken hostage. Trotsky managed to find 22,000 officers to command 330,000 men. He ruled the army with a fist of iron. In 1918 Trotsky issued orders promising death to deserters or to those who hid deserters. Shortly after these orders were issued, a Red Army battalion tried to run away from battle. Trotsky had one in ten of the soldiers executed by firing squad.

Trotsky was a brilliant military leader and spent much of the war travelling by train from one area to another, to direct operations and deliver supplies and encouragement. The Red Army became an effective and united fighting force which, by the end of 1919, was more than a match for the disunited Whites.

War Communism

While the civil war was progressing, there was an urgent need to feed the city workers and the Red Army as well as to introduce Communist ideas. The system used to try and achieve this was called **War Communism**. Factories with more than ten workers were controlled by the State and workers were subjected to military discipline. Private trade was banned so peasants had to give their surplus crops to the government and they could no longer sell them for profit. Food in the cities was strictly rationed. Money was allowed to lose its value and people were encouraged to barter.

War Communism did succeed in keeping the Red Army supplied with food and weapons.

How did Lenin organise the transition from Russian Empire to Soviet Union?

Although it had helped win the war, the policy of War Communism was failing because the peasants had decided that there was no point in growing more food than they needed for themselves – there was no incentive to do so as the government would take it away for nothing. After 1919, the peasants started to sow less grain and breed fewer animals. The result was a devastating famine. Seven million people died from starvation, disease and the cold weather. According to the Communists' own newspaper, a further 25 million Russians were living below the basic level of subsistence.

The civil war and War Communism combined to cause devastating hunger and famine.

In March 1921 there was a rising by the sailors at the Kronstadt Naval Base. The rising was put down, but Lenin realised that something would have to be done to prevent dissatisfaction spreading.

A major debate among Marxists before the revolution had been whether or not they should try to go straight to socialism and communism, or aim to take Russia through a capitalist stage. Lenin favoured the first method but became convinced that Russia had to go through some form of capitalism in order to develop. His answer to Russia's economic problems was the **New Economic Policy** (NEP).

The NEP said that:

Peasants would be allowed to sell their surplus food for profit once more.

Factories with fewer than twenty workers would be given back to their former owners.

Peasants who increased their food production would pay less tax.

People could use money again.

Many Bolsheviks disagreed with Lenin over this policy, fearing it was a step backwards. Lenin argued that it was necessary to take a step backwards so that the country could take two steps forward.

Improvement did take place, but not immediately, and despite the assistance of the American Relief Association, millions still died in 1921 and 1922. By 1925, the NEP started to achieve results and both food and industrial production began to increase dramatically.

> 'We hoped, through the decrees of the proletarian [workers] government, to found State industries and organise the distribution of State products upon a Communist basis in a country that was petit bourgeois [middle class/capitalist]. Life has shown we have made a mistake... you must attempt first to build small bridges which shall lead to a land of small peasant holdings through State Capitalism to Socialism. Otherwise you will never lead tens of millions of people to Communism.'
> **V. I. Lenin, 1921.**

This speech was one of many made by Lenin to try and justify the NEP. It was not only necessary to convince his own supporters – many of his opponents had argued these points before and had been shouted down by Lenin. No other country had gone through a Marxist revolution and Marx himself had predicted that the first countries to go through it would be advanced industrial nations, not backward ones like Russia.

At the beginning of 1923, old Russia was finally left behind with the introduction of a new name: **The Union of Soviet Socialist Republics** (USSR or Soviet Union), and a new constitution. The country was now a union of four republics – Russia, Byelorussia, the Ukraine and the Caucasus. Each republic controlled matters such as public health, welfare and education. The national government (Sovnarkom) controlled the armed forces, industry, communications and the secret police. The government was controlled by the **Communist Party** (as the Bolsheviks had called themselves since 1917).

Lenin was not to see much development of the USSR. The assassination attempt had weakened him and he had a series of strokes in 1922 and 1923. He died on 21 January 1924 leaving behind a power struggle as to who would replace him.

Lenin's Rule

1 The Economy 1913–1925

= *1913*   = *1922*   = *1925*

Grain harvest	Cattle	Electricity	Coal	Iron	Steel
80.1 / 50.3 / 72.5	58.9 / 45.8 / 72.5	1.9 / 0.8 / 2.9	29.0 / 9.5 / 18.1	4.2 / 0.1 / 1.5	4.3 / 0.4 / 2.1

Grain harvest
(millions of tonnes)

Cattle
(millions)

Electricity
(milliard Kw)

Coal
(millions of tonnes)

Iron
(millions of tonnes)

Steel
(millions of tonnes)

2 The Constituent Assembly

	Socialist Revolutionaries	370
	Bolsheviks	175
	Left Socialist Revolutionaries	40
	Cadets	17
	Mensheviks	16
	Others	89
	Total	707 votes

QUESTIONS

1   Write down the problems that Lenin and the Bolsheviks faced and explain how the actions they took began to solve each one of them.

2   Why did Lenin feel it necessary to disband the Constituent Assembly?

3   Look at the production statistics for 1913–1925 in the *Datapoint*. Do they prove that Lenin's War Communism ruined the country and his New Economic Policy rescued it?

4   Do you think that Leon Trotsky's organisation was the most important factor in the Bolsheviks winning the civil war? Explain you answer carefully.

5   How did Lenin strengthen his grip on the country? How might he have justified his actions?

Source Investigation

Lenin: man of the people or terrorist?

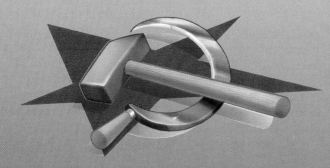

To his supporters Lenin was a great leader, wishing to be treated as an equal. To others he was a ruthless and cruel tyrant. Which view of him do you think is nearer the truth?

SOURCE B

'Lenin thought that all this terror was justified in such desperate circumstances. What did it matter if 50,000 died providing future generations enjoyed the benefits of Communism? Had he lived, Russia might have become a happier country, even if not a democratic one. Unfortunately he died in 1924.'

L.E. Snellgrove, writing in a school textbook in 1968.

SOURCE C

'until we apply terror —shooting on the spot — to speculators, we shall achieve nothing.'

Lenin, in 1918, justifying the use of the Cheka. He felt that like speculators, Constitutional Democrats, Mensheviks and Socialist Revolutionaries were also enemies of the State.

SOURCE A

'When congress met at 11.00 this morning, Kalinin was hardly able to speak and announced Lenin's death in a few broken sentences. Almost everyone in the great theatre burst into tears.... Tears were running down all faces... even the funeral march of the Revolutionaries was played by a weeping orchestra.'

Arthur Ransome, a British journalist recalling the reaction to Lenin's death.

SOURCE D

'In the Kremlin [government headquarters] he still occupied a small apartment built for a palace servant. In the recent winter, he like everyone else, had no heating. When he went to the barbers he took his turn, thinking it unseemly for anyone to give way to him. He knew that he was the Party's foremost brain and recently... had no more threat than that of resigning from the Central Committee....'

Serge, a fellow revolutionary, in 1920.

QUESTIONS

1   **What are the positive things Serge mentions about Lenin's character in Source D?**

2   **'Source A was written by a British journalist and therefore, it is a reliable account of the reaction to Lenin's death.' Do you agree? Explain you answer carefully.**

3   **What can you learn from Sources B and C about Lenin's view of the 'Red Terror'?**

4   **Source C is written by Lenin. Does this make the source more useful than the other sources?**

5   **'Lenin was just a ruthless dictator who simply wanted power for himself and his party.' Do these sources support this view? Give reasons for your answer.**

5 Stalin and the Modernisation of the USSR 1925–1941

Why did Stalin succeed Lenin?

Lenin died in January 1924. He had dominated the Bolsheviks for virtually a quarter of a century and had overshadowed the other leading Revolutionaries; could one man succeed him or was a group required? In all, there were seven men who were members of the **Politburo** (the most important committee of the Communist Party) who were possible successors to Lenin. Historians are fortunate, as Lenin wrote down what he thought of many of the leading Bolsheviks in 1922 in his Last Will and Testament.

'Comrade Stalin, having become Secretary [of the Party] has unlimited power in his hands, and I am not sure whether he will always be capable of using it with sufficient caution. Comrade Trotsky…is perhaps the most capable man in the present CC (Central Committee) but he has shown excessive preoccupation with the purely administrative side of the work.' [Post Script ten days later, January 1923] 'Stalin is too rude and this defect is intolerable in a General Secretary…. I suggest comrades think about a way of removing Stalin from his post and appointing another man who… [is] more tolerant, more loyal, more polite and more considerate to his colleagues…'

Extracts from Lenin's Last Will and Testament, December 1922

The Contestants

LEON TROTSKY

Post: Commissar of War.
Background and Experience: Had only become a Bolshevik in 1917. He had delivered many speeches against Lenin in his early days. Other Bolsheviks regarded him as an outsider. He was the military organiser of the Bolshevik Revolution. Trotsky was a brilliant tactician and the architect of the Red Army's victory in the civil war.
Personality: Brilliant intellect. Vain, arrogant and often contemptuous of colleagues.
Ideas: Disliked NEP. Wanted to send in 'shock brigades' to build new factories, power stations and railways.
Lenin's View: Excessively self-assured and preoccupied with administration.

GRIGORI ZINOVIEV

Post: Chairman of Communist International and Petrograd Soviet.
Background and Experience: A long-time Bolshevik. He had been in exile with Lenin in Switzerland and returned with him in April 1917. Showed leadership and organisational abilities.
Personality: Some vanity. Assumed he was Lenin's natural successor.
Ideas: Opposed NEP. Wanted rapid modernisation of industry. As Chairman of Comintern he supported the idea of 'exporting' revolution to Capitalist countries.
Lenin's view: Criticised by Lenin for not wholeheartedly supporting the Bolshevik Revolution.

LEON KAMENEV

Post: Chairman of the Politburo.
Background and Experience: A long-time Bolshevik. He had returned from exile to Russia before Lenin. Had been co-editor of Bolshevik newspaper *Pravda* (with Stalin). Acted as Lenin's deputy in many capacities.
Personality: Not always decisive. Would propose compromises.
Ideas: Opposed NEP and the support it gave to kulaks. He felt money for modernising the USSR could come from taxing the peasants.
Lenin's View: Criticised for proposing co-operation with the Provisional Government in March 1917 and for questioning whether the Bolsheviks were ready to take over in October 1917.

JOSEPH STALIN

Posts: General Secretary of the Party, Member of the Organisation Bureau (in charge of Party organisation), Head of the Control Commission (in charge of the Party's membership) and Commissar for Nationalities (having control over the republics of the USSR).

Background and Experience: A long-time Bolshevik. Organised bank raids in early days to support Party funds. Co-editor of *Pravda* on return to Petrograd from exile in March 1917. Played minor part in Bolshevik Revolution.

Ideas: Supported Lenin and tried to give the impression that he was Lenin's pupil. Believed USSR should be modernised before revolution could be 'exported' – called this view 'Socialism in One Country'.

Lenin's View: Felt he was too rude and would not know how to use his authority with restraint. Suggested replacing him with someone more tolerant and loyal. (While Lenin was ill, Stalin had been abusive to Lenin's wife, who complained that no other Party member had ever been rude to her.)

NIKOLAI BUKHARIN

Post: In charge of press and propaganda.
Background and Experience: A long-time Bolshevik. Great theorist and respected writer. Had played a part in the Revolution. Had opposed the peace treaty with Germany.
Personality: Respected by theorists. Not always diplomatic or good at political tactics.
Ideas: Supported NEP. Wanted to support the peasants and believed that building them up was a key to supporting future industrial development.
Lenin's View: Lenin was not convinced about Bukharin's commitment to Marxism but did not feel this should be held against him.

ANDREI RYKOV

Post: Chairman of Sovnarkom (Cabinet).
Background and Experience: A long-time Bolshevik. Had wanted to co-operate with other socialist groups in 1917. Resigned from office when Lenin would not form a coalition with other socialists in November 1917 but returned later. Frequently acted as Lenin's deputy.
Personality: Not outstanding or dynamic.
Ideas: Supported NEP.
Lenin's View: Little mention of him in Lenin's Last Will and Testament.

MIKHAIL TOMSKY

Post: In charge of trade unions.
Background and Experience: A long-time Bolshevik. One of the few working men amongst the leaders of the Bolshevik Party.
Personality: Not seen as being forceful or dynamic.
Ideas: Supported NEP.
Lenin's View: Little mentioned.

QUESTIONS

1 **For these possible successors to Lenin, write down the positive points which would make each a good leader and the negative points which would make each a bad leader.**

2 **Who would you choose as Lenin's successor? Explain your answer carefully.**

3 **Who would you not choose as Lenin's successor? Explain you answer carefully.**

4 **Regardless of who you would prefer to win, who is the most likely candidate? Why?**

The Contest

ZINOVIEV   TROTSKY   KAMENEV   STALIN   BUKHARIN   RYKOV   TOMSKY

The contest for the leadership had, in fact, begun when Lenin had a stroke at the end of 1922 and it became obvious that he would never completely recover. Trotsky probably regarded himself as the natural successor. His abilities, however, made the others jealous and since he had only become a Bolshevik in 1917, the rest of the Politburo, in particular Zinoviev, Kamenev and Stalin, combined to prevent him from taking power. By the time of Lenin's death, Trotsky was effectively out of the contest. He later claimed that Stalin tricked him by giving him the wrong date for Lenin's funeral. While the others, especially Stalin, were mourning and declaring eternal loyalty to Lenin's ideas, Trotsky was on sick leave in the south of the USSR. Trotsky's only hope would have been to appeal to the Party or raise a revolt, but his own theories on Party loyalty prevented him from doing so.

ZINOVIEV   TROTSKY   KAMENEV   STALIN   BUKHARIN   RYKOV   TOMSKY

Although they disliked Trotsky, Zinoviev and Kamenev did agree with his political and economic views. They were known as the 'Left Opposition'. They wanted to achieve socialism in the USSR by encouraging revolutions in other countries. If the whole of Europe underwent a revolution, then the future for socialism would be safe. Their views also favoured ending NEP which they felt supported the peasant at the expense of industry. In its place they would concentrate their efforts on planning the economy and building up the industrial strength of the USSR.

Stalin developed an alternative view called 'Socialism in One Country' in which he said that the needs of the rest of the world should take second place to the needs of the USSR. He felt that if the USSR built a modern and prosperous economy then Capitalist nations would never dare attack the USSR. With the support of Bukharin, Tomsky and Rykov (the 'Rightists'), Stalin's views were pushed forward and the policies of the others were attacked. At the end of 1925 Zinoviev and Kamenev were defeated at the Communist Party Congress. Soon afterwards, they along with Trotsky, were dismissed from the Politburo and in 1927, Zinoviev and Trotsky were expelled from the Party.

QUESTIONS

1 **Why might Lenin's Last Will and Testament have dealt a devastating blow to Stalin had it been published?**

2 **How did Stalin's views on the economy change in this period? Suggest reasons for these changes.**

3 **How far would you agree with the view that Stalin's rise to supreme power was entirely due to his own ruthless determination? Give your explanation in a detailed answer.**

ROUND 2

ZINOVIEV	TROTSKY	KAMENEV	STALIN	BUKHARIN	RYKOV	TOMSKY

If Lenin's view of Stalin had been revealed, then perhaps Stalin's candidature would have been over as quickly as Trotsky's. Yet he was saved by two things. Firstly, Lenin's view was not complimentary about any of the possible successors, so the Politburo decided not to publish it to the Party as a whole. Secondly, when it was read out to the Central Committee of the Communist Party, Zinoviev said that Stalin had worked in perfect harmony with Kamenev and himself and therefore, although right about most things, Lenin had been wrong about Stalin.

ROUND 4

ZINOVIEV	TROTSKY	KAMENEV	STALIN	BUKHARIN	RYKOV	TOMSKY

The places of Zinoviev, Kamenev and Trotsky in the Politburo were taken by Stalin's supporters. Stalin now turned against the Rightists. He argued that NEP had done its work and that it was time to abandon it in favour of building up the USSR's industry and modernising its economy. He proposed rigorous planning and an almost military approach to the organising of labour. The Rightists tried to argue against him but Stalin now held the majority in the Politburo and won all the arguments. Bukharin, Rykov and Tomsky tried to call on the Left Opposition for help but many of them now, temporarily at least, offered support to Stalin. The Rightists were first stripped of their posts and then their positions in the Politburo. Effective opposition to Stalin was over.

The Victory

ZINOVIEV	TROTSKY	KAMENEV	STALIN	BUKHARIN	RYKOV	TOMSKY

By 1929 Stalin was supreme leader of the USSR. All sections of the Party were in his control or run by his supporters who depended on him for their positions. Gradually at first, but with increasing pace, he used his powers to eliminate all possible opposition.

Why did Stalin introduce the Five-Year Plans and collectivisation?

By 1928, the Soviet economy had almost recovered to its pre-1914 position. However, Russia had been so far behind the other nations that it was not necessarily a notable achievement. In fact, since the war, the Capitalist countries had made even more advances. NEP had begun to introduce capitalism on a small scale to try and 'kick-start' the economy and prepare the USSR for socialism, but there were doubts as to its success.

1

'To achieve the victory of socialism in one country we need to catch up and overtake these countries in the technical and economic sense. Either we do it or we shall be crushed.'

Stalin in a speech in 1928 explaining the need for modernisation.

2

'The tempo [speed] must not be reduced... To slacken the tempo would mean falling behind. And those who fall behind get beaten. No, we refuse to be beaten! One feature of the old Russia was the continual beatings she suffered for falling behind, for her backwardness.... Do you want our socialist fatherland to be beaten and to lose its independence? If you do not want this you must put an end to its backwardness in the shortest possible time.... We are fifty to a hundred years behind the advanced countries. We must make good this distance in ten years. Either we do it, or they crush us.'

Stalin in 1931 explaining why the targets of his plans should be achieved in four years rather then five.

3

This poster shows the achievements of Stalin's modernisation programme despite foreign enemies. The writing in Russian is a quotation from Stalin:

'With the banner of Lenin we achieved decisive successes in the victory of socialist construction. With this same banner we shall conquer the proletarian revolution throughout the world.'

4

Russia 1913. Industrial output compared to the USA and UK.

Coal	One-17th of USA	One-10th of UK
Oil	One-3rd of USA	
Steel	One-8th of USA	One-Half of UK

The problems

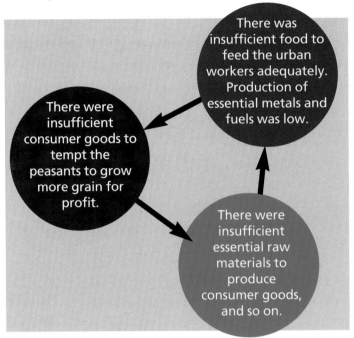

There was insufficient food to feed the urban workers adequately. Production of essential metals and fuels was low.

There were insufficient consumer goods to tempt the peasants to grow more grain for profit.

There were insufficient essential raw materials to produce consumer goods, and so on.

The solutions

Stalin could not wait for these improvements to happen naturally. He demanded improvement immediately and he set out to do this through the **Five-Year Plans**.

Stalin's great plan for agriculture was called **collectivisation**. Farms were to join together and their land and resources were to be pooled. This went against the individual ownership that the peasants had fought for, and threatened the prosperity of the **kulaks** (richer peasants). Many resisted. Nevertheless, as a result of collectivisation, new machinery and tractors began to appear and better facilities such as hospitals and schools were developed on some collective farms. Collectivisation took longer to be put in place across the USSR than Stalin had expected.

With advice from his economists, Stalin set production targets for each area of industry to achieve. The first Five-Year Plan began in October 1928, but in 1929 Stalin decreed the targets were to be achieved in four years. As soon as this period was up, a second Five-Year Plan for 1932–1937 was drawn up. Workers were constantly urged to achieve their targets which were displayed on huge posters in town centres throughout the Soviet Union.

What improvements were needed?

FUEL

Production of coal, oil and electricity essential to power the USSR's industrial revolution.

RAW MATERIALS

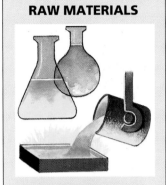

Iron, steel, chemicals, textiles to make basic goods and machines.

MACHINERY

To make goods for consumers and provide the means of transport.

AGRICULTURE

To feed the workers and to sell grain to help finance some of the industrial changes.

The Five-Year Plans

1 Map of USSR showing centres of heavy industry

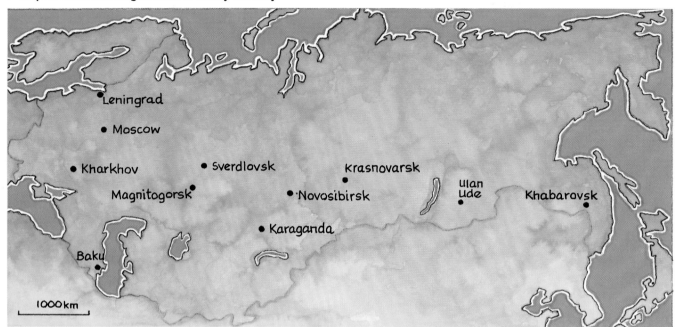

Stalin was advised in his planning by two state agencies – Veshenka and Gosplan. Part of the advice he received was to build up centres of heavy industry – in some cases completely from scratch. Two of the most famous were Magnitogorsk and Sverdlovsk in the Ural Mountains. Both of which had been virtually non-existent before the Five-Year Plans.

Sverdlovsk

Like Magnitogorsk, Sverdlovsk experienced rapid change. These pictures show an impressive development, but you should bear in mind that they were officially produced by Stalin's government to show how successful his policies were. The second photograph gives you only an impression of one small part of Sverdlovsk and neither photo gives any indication of the quality or quantity of goods produced.

Magnitogorsk

1929 - *Population:* 1157 *Amenities:* tumble-down houses and open sewers

1933 - *Population:* 100,000 *Amenities:* hospital, school, shops, factories, mills and blast furnaces

2 Production of raw materials in the First and Second Five-Year Plans

Estimates by British historian Alec Nove of industrial output in millions of tonnes.

	1927–28	1932–33		1937	
		(Planned)	(Actual)	(Planned)	(Actual)
OIL	11.7	22.0	21.4	46.8	28.5
STEEL	4.0	10.4	5.9	17.0	17.7
COAL	35.4	75.0	64.3	152.5	128.0

3 Production of USSR, USA and UK (1913 and 1940)

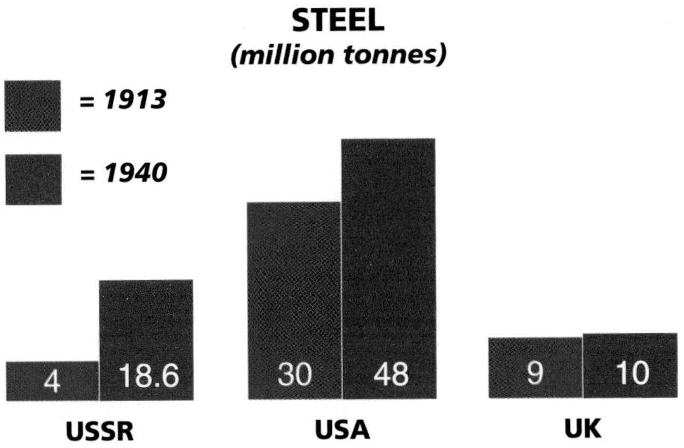

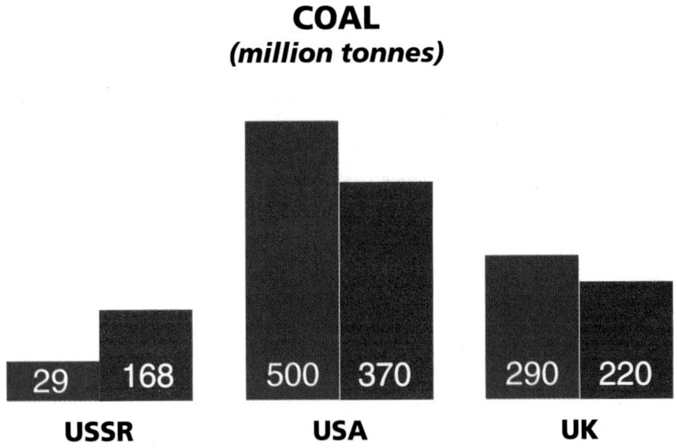

STEEL
(million tonnes)

= *1913*

= *1940*

USSR	USA	UK
4 18.6	30 48	9 10

COAL
(million tonnes)

USSR	USA	UK
29 168	500 370	290 220

From 1929 until the outbreak of World War II, Capitalist countries were affected by a world-wide economic depression.

= *1913*   = *1929*   = *1938*

4 Production of Secondary Industries 1913–1938 in the USSR

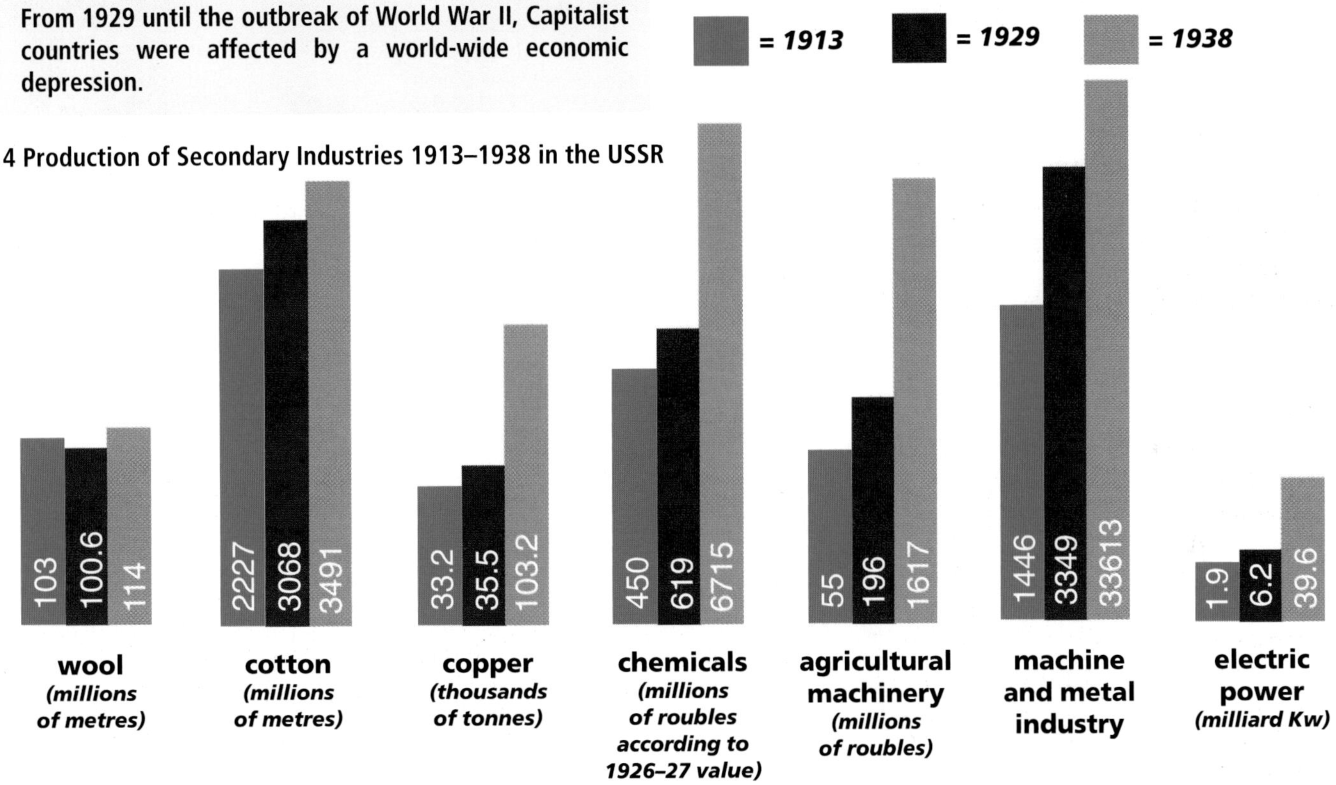

wool *(millions of metres)*	cotton *(millions of metres)*	copper *(thousands of tonnes)*	chemicals *(millions of roubles according to 1926–27 value)*	agricultural machinery *(millions of roubles)*	machine and metal industry	electric power *(milliard Kw)*
103 100.6 114	2227 3068 3491	33.2 35.5 103.2	450 619 6715	55 196 1617	1446 3349 33613	1.9 6.2 39.6

Q U E S T I O N S

1. How was industry affected by Stalin's Five-Year Plans? Give as many supporting details as possible.

2. In many cases the targets were not achieved. Does this mean that the Five-Year Plans were a failure? Give reasons for your answer.

3. The statistics in this *Datapoint* are either from official government figures or from estimates by non-Soviet historians. In what ways does this affect the reliability and usefulness of the statistics?

4. This information focuses on industrial development, output and performance. What else would you need to consider before deciding whether or not Stalin's Five-Year Plans benefited the USSR?

Collectivisation

Stalin's plan for agriculture was to bring together the various small, inefficient farms and form large, mechanised and efficient collective farms or **kolkhoz**.

The peasants were required to hand over most of their land to the kolkhoz which was to be managed by a committee elected by the local Communist Party.

Each kolkhoz was set an annual production target by Stalin's planners. The diagram below (source 1) shows the distribution of the produce of the kolkhoz.

Stalin believed that the enemies of a successful agricultural policy were the richer peasants, or kulaks. To many peasants, collectivisation seemed to be taking them back to the serfdom (slavery) of Tsarist Russia and so there was much opposition to it (see Source 3).

1

40%
to buy seeds, and so on

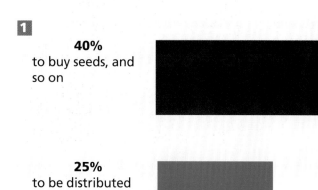

25%
to be distributed amongst the peasants as wages

15%
to be given to the machine tractor station which supplied each collective with its machinery

15%
to be given to the government at a fixed lower price

5%
to be given to the government at a higher price

Each member of the kolkhoz was allowed to keep their home, a few tools, a few animals and a small vegetable plot.

2

Peasants at a kolkhoz.

3

'The woman... held a flaming sheaf of grain in her hands. Before anyone could reach her, she had tossed the burning sheaf onto the thatched roof of her house, which burst into flames instantaneously. "Infidels! Murderers!" the distraught woman was shrieking. "We worked all our lives for our house. You won't have it. The flames will have it."'

Victor Kravchenko describing the reaction of a peasant, probably a kulak, to collectivisation in his book, *I Chose Freedom*, (1946).

The novelist Mikhail Sholokhov wrote of peasants slaughtering their animals and eating meat until they were 'drunk' to prevent the collective taking their stock.

All who stood against collectivisation were denounced as kulaks. At best the kulaks were the targets of aggressive propaganda, at worst they were deported, imprisoned or exterminated. Troops were sent into the countryside to seize the produce and livestock that the peasants refused to give up.

In this cartoon the kulak is seen on his fertile plot (in the background), self-satisfied and unaware of the needs of those around him. This portrayal was intended to encourage the jealousy and hatred of the ordinary peasants towards the wealthy farmers.

The stubbornness of the peasants' attitude to collectivisation, combined with policy mistakes and Stalin's ruthless methods to force acceptance, caused famine. The novelist, Victor Kravchenko, described a situation where peasants were eating 'everything we could lay our hands on – cats, dogs, the field mice, birds.' Peasants would even fight over horse manure in case they could find whole grains in it. Not surprisingly, many died.

These peasants are at a meeting to hear about the benefits of collectivisation from a Communist Party worker. The poster in the middle says: 'Batrak – Go to the Kolkhoz'. Batraks were the poorest of the peasants with no land of their own. It was easier to convince them of the advantages of the kolkhoz.

The Effects of Collectivisation

1 Food production in the USSR 1928–1932

		1928	1929	1930	1931	1932
Grain *(million tonnes)*		73.3	71.7	83.5	69.5	69.6
Cattle *(millions)*		70.5	67.1	52.5	47.9	40.7
Pigs *(millions)*		26.0	20.4	13.6	14.4	11.6
Sheep and goats *(millions)*		146.7	147.0	108.8	77.7	52.1

2 Animals slaughtered by peasants 1929–1933

- **16 million out of 34 million horses**
- **30 million out of 60 million cattle**
- **100 million sheep and goats**

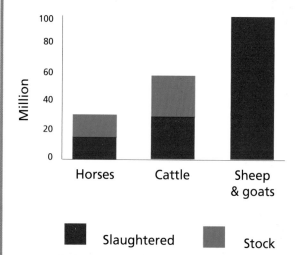

Slaughtered ▪   Stock ▪

3 Death toll amongst peasants 1930–37

1932–33 Famine

Ukraine:	**5 million**
North Caucasus:	**1 million**
elsewhere:	**1 million**

De-kulakisation

USSR:	**6.5 million**

Stalin had felt his policy would prevent starvation; instead it seemed to make it worse. Despite the apparent overall failure, individual kolkhoz were often successful and did in fact bring many benefits to the peasants in terms of their living and material conditions.

Q U E S T I O N S

1. **How successful was collectivisation? Give details to support your answer.**

2. **What was the main cause of famine, Stalin's policy or the attitude of the peasants? Give reasons for your answer considering both points of view.**

How were the Soviet people affected by Stalin's economic policies?

The high targets set by the Soviet planners demanded almost military discipline. 'Absenteeism' was described as more than one day off work without good reason and was punished with dismissal and eviction from factory housing. In 1938, this was changed to absenteeism being more than twenty minutes late without good reason. In addition, to prevent workers moving around trying to find better jobs, internal passports were introduced. No one could move without the secret police – the OGPU – knowing. Workers also carried work books listing their previous jobs as well as any offences committed against labour disciplines.

In 1929 weavers in one factory complained of having to work four shifts and having nothing in the way of basic necessities, for example, shoes and clothing to spend their meagre wages on. Yet in many ways, these workers could count themselves lucky. A large number of the new towns, factories, dams and bridges were built by those held in labour camps – Stalin's opponents, kulaks, factory absentees and members of religious organisations.

This Soviet poster proclaims: 'The development of a network of créches, kindergartens, canteens and laundries will ensure that women take part in socialist construction'. It gives the impression of a well-looked-after workforce, happy in their labours. The reality was that in most cases, the Soviet citizen in towns and in the country had little to be happy about.

Slave Labour

There were prison camps throughout the Soviet Union. Political prisoners put to work on this construction site received the equivalent of 20p a month for working 18 hours a day, seven days a week. Whereas Western Capitalist countries used machines to aid construction, the Soviets used hard manual labour almost exclusively.

Numbers held in prison camps 1929–1938

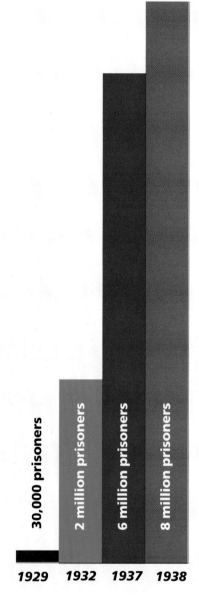

30,000 prisoners	2 million prisoners	6 million prisoners	8 million prisoners
1929	*1932*	*1937*	*1938*

'The newly-arrived transport saw... [that] every tent in the settlement was surrounded with piles of frozen corpses on three out of four sides, except where the door was.'

Alexander Solzhenitsyn writing about the Orutukan camp in the winter of 1937–38. Solzhenitsyn was imprisoned in a number of camps. He wrote about his experiences after Stalin's death. He was later expelled from the USSR.

There were those who approved of the new work practices in the Soviet Union. Young Communists, in particular, formed 'shock brigades' which set out to invigorate industry and achieve targets by competing with each other and ensuring that they were never absent from work. These workers received higher pay, better conditions and better housing, and they could expect to receive privileges like tickets to the theatre, paid holidays and access to special shops selling goods not generally available. The very best workers, the **Stakhanovites**, were given hero status and medals. They were named after the miner Stakhanov, who dug 102 tonnes of coal in a single shift instead of the usual seven tonnes.

Other miners, car workers, shoemakers, soon became medal-holding 'Heroes of Socialist Labour' and some were given new flats at a time when good housing was scarce. They were, however, sometimes badly treated by their fellow-workers and a few were even murdered. In the late 1930s, the Stakhanov movement was quietly dropped.

Many of the workers in the new industrial towns were peasants. As hard as some of them tried, it was difficult for them to adjust. In some industries where precision was required, barely literate workers still used their fingers for measurement. John Scott, an American engineer who worked in Magnitogorsk wrote:

'...*Khaibulin, the Tartar, had never seen a staircase, a locomotive or an electric light until he had come to Magnitogorsk a year before.... Now Khaibulin was building a blast furnace bigger than any in Europe....*'

Despite the hardships, Stalin was able to point to better schools, hospitals, clinics, crèches, housing, central heating, improved transportation as real achievements even if they did elude many workers. In the USA during the 1930s, unemployment reached fifteen million, with many queuing for charity bread handouts. By contrast, in the USSR everyone had a job.

Stakhanov is shown here shortly after achieving his record. The Soviet citizen was told of the heroic Stakhanov's efficiency but not informed that he was given the best seam to work, the most modern equipment to use, and unskilled assistants to carry the coal away for him.

QUESTIONS

1 What benefits did some Soviet workers receive?

2 What difficulties faced many who worked in the USSR?

3 How were the Soviet people affected by the economic changes introduce by Stalin?

4 'By modernising Soviet industry, Stalin made the USSR a better place to live.'

Using information given in this chapter, show in detail how this view can be supported and how it can be challenged.

5 'In industry Stalin succeeded, but in agriculture he failed.' Is this a fair description of Stalin's economic policies? Explain your answer carefully.

How successful were Stalin's economic policies?

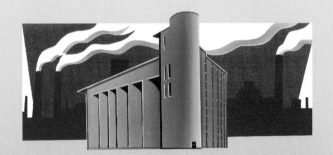

SOURCE A

'You accuse us of making false promises... Last year you got a schoolhouse, and have you forgotten how we of the Party and of the Soviet had to squeeze out of you through the voluntary tax your share of the cost of the schoolhouse? And now? Aren't you glad your children can attend school?... Were we wrong when we urged you to build a fire station?... Were we wrong when we urged you to lay decent bridges across your stream in the swamp? Were we wrong when we threatened to fire you if you didn't take home two loads of peat to mix with the bedding for your stock so as to have good fertiliser?'

The organiser of a kolkhoz answering criticisms from one of its members.

SOURCE B

'In 1938 though the city [of Magnitogorsk] was still a primitive state... it did boast 50 schools, 3 colleges, 2 large theatres, half a dozen small ones, 17 libraries, 22 clubs, 18 clinics....

The city of Magnitogorsk grew and developed from the dirty, chaotic construction camp of the early thirties into a reasonably healthy and habitable city....

New stores were built and supplies of all kinds made their appearance in quantity and at reasonable prices. Fuel, clothing of all kinds, and other elementary necessities became available.'

John Scott, describing his work at Magnitogorsk in his book *Life behind the Urals.*

SOURCE C

'[The room] was furnished after a style, the usual divan up against one wall, table, chairs, no wardrobe.... We were led down to the communal kitchen in the basement... "My" section consisted of an upended packing case and two reeking kerosene stoves. On these I was expected to cook, boil up washing and heat water for an occasional bath taken in the room above... The room was good for Moscow, we were assured. At least we would not have to share with another family.'

Betty Rowland, *Caviare for Breakfast* (1979). Betty was a Australian who lived in Moscow from January 1933 to August 1934.

SOURCE D

'We went to inspect the farm buildings. First we visited the restaurant which was in an old and somewhat dilapidated main building, with places for about forty people at small tables. Most of the peasants were awfully poor looking. They were drinking a soup which appeared to be quite nourishing.

We then went to the village club, a wooden building which had a small meeting hall as well as a tiny library. There were pictures of tractors showing the spare parts, and pictures showing how necessary it was for the peasants to work steadily instead of lazing their time away and not attending their crops.'

Walter Citrine, *I Search for Truth in Russia*. Walter Citrine was the leader of the British Trade Union movement. He visited the USSR in 1936.

SOURCE E

Peasants were murdered by Communists and whole villages were sometimes wiped out under Stalin's de-kulakisation. Why then, do you think so many people were willing to pose for this photograph?

QUESTIONS

1. Look at Sources A, B and D. What benefits did Stalin's policies bring the Soviet people?

2. Look at Sources A and E. What prospects faced those who stood in the way of Stalin's policies?

3. There is no date given for the photograph in Source E. How does this affect its usefulness?

4. In what ways is Betty Rowland's evidence (Source C) useful in showing that Stalin's modernisation of Russia did not improve the lives of the Soviet people?

5. As a Trade Unionist, Walter Citrine (Source D) would have supported socialism. Does this make his evidence unreliable? Explain your answer carefully.

6. 'Stalin's policies resulted in hardship and persecution for the ordinary Soviet people.' Do these sources provide support for that view? Give a detailed answer making appropriate reference to Sources A to E.

6 Denounced – Khrushchev's Verdict on Stalin

Was Stalin a tyrant or a genius?

The sources on this page are differing views of Stalin. Can you decide which is true? How useful are each of these sources? How reliable are they? Taken together they give a more complete picture. Stalin was responsible for the deaths of thousands, he was cruel and hungry for power and yet he did modernise and transform the Soviet State, ultimately improving the lives of many. In trying to analyse the benefits of Stalin's modernisation in its obituary, *The Guardian* said:

> *'It is hard to say whether the same result could be achieved at less cost. But the cost was certainly exorbitant....'*

Part of the job of a historian is to decide whether the cost was justified or not.

1

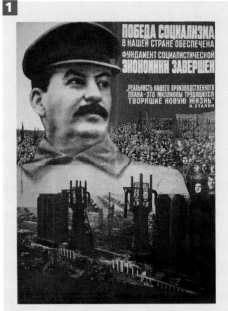

On 6 March 1953, Joseph Stalin died at the age of 74.

2

> *'The heart of Joseph Vissarionovich Stalin – Lenin's Comrade in arms and the Genius-endowed Continuer of his work, Wise Leader and Teacher of the Communist Party and of the Soviet People – has ceased to beat.'*

The announcement of Stalin's death on Soviet Radio at 4 am on 6 March 1953.

3

> *'[Under Stalin]...arrest and deportation on a massive scale...executions without trial or explanation, created conditions of insecurity, fear and even despair.... Several thousand honest and innocent communists died as a result of gross distortion of the facts.'*

Extracts from Khrushchev's speech to the Twentieth Congress of the Communist Party in 1956. Khrushchev was Stalin's successor. The speech was intended to be a secret but was 'leaked' to the West.

4

> *'Stalin found Russia working with a wooden plough and left her with atomic piles... Lenin had denied freedom to the old ruling classes and their parties, but he hoped that the working classes would enjoy the fullest economic and social liberty in the new State.... Stalin turned that State into an autocracy.'*

Isaac Deutscher in his obituary of Stalin, 6 March 1953.

5

> *'O'er the earth the rising sun sheds a warmer light,
> Since it looked on Stalin's face it has grown more bright.
> I am singing to my baby sleeping in my arms...
> ...You will learn the source of sunshine bathing all our land.
> You will copy Stalin's portrait with your tiny hand.'*

The composer Prokoviev writing to celebrate Stalin's 60th birthday in 1939. Quoted in **J. Laver**, *Joseph Stalin: from Revolutionary to Despot* (1993).

6

> *'Stalin transformed Russia from a backward country into one of the two greatest Powers in the world, with its industrial and intellectual resources multiplied many times over. He brought it safely through a terrible war.'*

An extract from *The Guardian's* obituary of Stalin, 6 March 1953.

Why did Khrushchev denounce Stalin?

This question can be examined in two ways:
1 Why did Khrushchev want to denounce Stalin?
2 What were his accusations based upon?

The answer to the first question is political. When Lenin died there had been no obvious single successor. When Stalin died there was a similar situation. For some time there was collective leadership under Malenkov, Molotov and Khrushchev. In seeking to concentrate all power into his own hands, Khrushchev tried to set himself apart from the others. This he did by denouncing Stalin's methods and personality (though he had himself worked under Stalin and supported his ideas of central control).

Khrushchev appeared moderate and dynamic, while his rivals seemed to be allied to Stalin and the past. The strategy worked and Khrushchev was able to assume supreme leadership from 1957 to 1964.

The motives for Khrushchev's accusations can be questioned, but when the second question is investigated, it can be seen that they were based on real evidence. If Stalin had been put on trial before his death, the charges would have probably read as follows:

1

In pushing through his Five-Year Plans, millions of people faced hardship, overwork, imprisonment or death. By 1938 there were eight million prisoners in labour camps.

2

In collectivising agriculture, six and a half million died as a result of de-kulakisation and at least seven million died from famine.

3

He invented the term 'enemy of the people' and applied it to anyone who might be a rival. Millions were 'purged'. By 1938 over a fifth of the Communist Party had been shot or expelled. Leading Bolsheviks who had been active in the Revolution such as Zinoviev, Kamanev, Rykov and Bukharin were executed. By 1939 every admiral, three of five Red Army marshals, and roughly half the officers of the armed forces had been shot.

4

He developed the 'Cult of Personality'; he was worshipped as Lenin's successor and a genius in his own right. All art and literature reflected his 'greatness' and all writing and broadcasting was censored, and contained only his views.

Why did Stalin launch the purges and the 'Cult of Personality'?

From the time he came to power, Stalin never really felt secure. Perhaps it was because his own rise to power had been underhand, or perhaps he feared the greater intellectual capabilities of those he had outwitted. Whatever the reason, it was in his interest to remove all opposition.

The 'purges' began in 1934 with the murder of Sergei Kirov, the chairman of the Leningrad Soviet and the most popular member of the Party – in other words, a potential rival. Much evidence points to Stalin's involvement in the murder. Stalin showed his cunning, however, by accusing his other rivals of organising the murder and they were brought to trial. Events then moved quickly.

Spring 1935

Thousands in Leningrad imprisoned or shot after being accused of conspiring to murder Kirov.

Summer 1936

The first 'show trial', the Trial of the Sixteen. Zinoviev, Kamenev and fourteen others are convicted of conspiring with Trotsky to overthrow the government. All but one are shot.

January 1937

The Trial of the Seventeen. The accused are found guilty of conspiring with Trotsky to wreck industry and form terrorist groups. All found guilty, thirteen shot.

In the same year Marshal Tukhachevsky, the USSR's most distinguished soldier, together with seven generals are executed without trial for 'espionage and treason'.

1939

Those disposed of include leading officials, secretaries to the Party, members of the Communist Youth Organisation, foreign communists, writers, factory managers, engineers and scientists.

March 1938

The Trial of the Twenty-One. Bukharin, Rykov and nineteen others found guilty of conspiring with Trotsky to wreck industry and helping foreign spies. All found guilty and shot.

In the same year Yagoda, the head of the secret police, the NKVD, confessed to murdering his predecessor, assisting in Kirov's murder, planning a military takeover, admitting foreign spies into the secret police and planning to murder the whole Politburo.

1940

Trotsky murdered by one of Stalin's agents whilst in exile in Mexico.

'He [Stalin] is unhappy at not being able to convince everyone, himself included, that he is greater than anyone else; and this unhappiness of his may be his most human trait, perhaps the only human trait in him. But what is not human... is that because of this unhappiness he cannot avoid taking revenge on people.... If someone speaks better then he does, that man is for it! Stalin will not let him live, because that man is a constant reminder that he, Stalin, is not the first and the best.... he [Stalin] is a narrow-minded, malicious man – no not a man, but a devil.'

Nikolai Bukharin speaking to Fyodor Dan, a Menshevik, in Paris in 1936. Bukharin was executed under Stalin's orders in 1938.

Was there real opposition to Stalin? With Stalin controlling the newspapers and radio, it is difficult to determine whether the threats were real or simply in his imagination. What is certain is that with each purge, his position grew even stronger and fewer people were inclined to deny him their devotion. If there was no real opposition, how can we account for so many confessing to their crimes?

'Confessions' could be extracted through a variety of methods. Some victims were told that their families or friends were under threat if they did not confess. Others were broken down in interrogation, some were told that confession would shorten their sentence and some simply confessed because they thought that to do so was in the best interests of the Party.

Stalin created an atmosphere of fear in which the only safe thing to do was to support him. The Soviet citizen had to be careful about what he or she said and to whom he or she said it. Particular care had to be taken to avoid being associated with Trotsky.

1

The majority of Stalin's victims were imprisoned or shot without trial. However, the most important public figures were given 'show trials' as a warning to others. These trials gave the defendants little hope of real justice as most 'confessed' to their 'crimes' anyway.

2

'.... [Bukharin] was a child of his time, a child of the [Communist] Party, he was devoted to it.... It explains his capitulation [surrender]; he thought that it was in the interests of the Party.'

From J. Lewis and P. Whitehead, *Stalin: A Time for Judgement* (1991).

3

'The interrogators worked in shifts; I didn't. Seven days without food or sleep, without even returning to my cell.... The object... is to wear out the nerves, weaken the body, break the resistance, and force the prisoner to sign whatever is required.'

This is the account of Eugenia Ginzburg explaining why she 'confessed'. She was arrested and tried in 1937 and given a ten-year sentence which she spent in a number of labour camps. She was released in 1955.

4

'On June 22, 1936, a portrait of Trotsky was discovered in the living quarters of Afaanasiya Uromova... a corrupt member of the kolkhoz who carried on subversive work in the kolkhoz... I request that measures be taken to investigate and bring Uromova to trial.'

A note sent to a member of the secret police.

5

This cartoon is attacking Trotsky. The verse beneath it says: 'The hero of crimes and treachery, Does not forget the rules of hygiene. Those who are in the pay of fascists [right-wing opponents of Communism, e.g. the Nazis], Live by scientific rules. The executioner, finishing his day's work, Washes his hands in fear.'

Trotsky is shown here working for the German Nazis. Notice how grotesque he has been made to look to further frighten the Soviet people.

'The genius of our age'

1

Christmas 1949. The image of Stalin is projected on to the underside of the clouds. Whilst creating fear in the minds of his people, Stalin carefully developed the idea that only he could save the USSR from all that threatened it. Statues of Stalin were everywhere. He was described in the newspapers (all controlled by him) as the 'Universal Genius', the 'Man of Steel' (the name 'Stalin' means 'man of steel'), and other outrageously flattering titles.

Stalin, who for much of the 1920s and 1930s attacked religion, allowed himself to be worshipped like a god. His life was celebrated in plays, poems, stories and novels.

4

Lenin and Stalin in August 1922. Stalin used photographs such as this to show himself as Lenin's natural successor. Many photographs were falsified by having Stalin superimposed. Other Bolsheviks, especially Trotsky, were removed from photographs and paintings.

2

Stalin's teachings were in the Short Course on the History of the CPSU (the Communist Party), which became the staple diet of every school child and student in the country. There it was shown how the Bolshevik Party under the leadership of Lenin, with his disciple Stalin at this side, had carried out the October Revolution.... All other Bolshevik leaders... were characterised as splitters, saboteurs or traitors who had done their best to impede the course chosen by the two great men. This was a simple-minded, mythical account of Soviet history, with its straightforward heroes and villains.'

G. Hosking, *A History of the Soviet Union* (1990).

3

Stalin exploited the education system to build up his image and his version of events. The following account was written by the poet **Nadezdha Mandelstram** after speaking to a schoolgirl. It shows the way schoolbooks were changed to show whatever 'truth' Stalin wanted to be known at the time.

'Varia... showed us her school textbooks where the portraits of the party leaders had thick pieces of paper pasted over them as one by one they fell into disgrace – this the children had to do on instructions from their teacher.... With every new arrest people went through their books and burned the works of disgraced leaders in their stoves. In new apartment buildings, which had central heating instead of stoves, forbidden books, personal diaries, correspondence and other "subversive" literature had to be cut up in pieces and thrown down the toilet.'

All newspapers were under the control of Stalin as was art, literature and music. All aspects of culture were expected to show 'socialist realism', that is, to deal with ordinary working people and to show the progress of Communism. The progress of Communism and the genius of Stalin were the same thing.

The 1936 Constitution

In 1936 Stalin introduced a new constitution. On the face of it, it liberalised life in the USSR, allowing freedom of speech, of conscience, of the press and of meeting. A Supreme Soviet would be directly elected by everyone of eighteen and over in a secret ballot. The reality was that there was no freedom, Stalin dominated everything. The Supreme Soviet met for only two weeks a year. The ruling committee of the Party, the Praesidium, controlled by Stalin, had the real power.

6

5

The USSR had become a totalitarian state with Stalin dominating everything. This photograph shows one of many parades celebrating his glory.

Both of these posters show examples of 'socialist realism'. In the first one, Stalin is urging the workers to march towards progress with him. In the second, the Soviet people are illustrated as soldiers against those who might try to exploit the Soviet Union (e.g. the Capitalist countries who Stalin claimed were being helped by Trotsky and his supporters). 'Socialist realism' was intended to appeal to the hearts and minds of the workers, ignoring the usual artistic and intellectual aspects of culture. Stalin was not intellectually aloof like the disgraced Bolsheviks; he stood alongside his workers.

Stalin and the Purges

1

This cartoon was drawn up by an opponent of Stalin's whilst in exile in Paris. The caption reads 'Visit the USSR's Pyramids...' The 'pyramids' are formed from the skulls of those who died in the purges. The original pyramids are seen as Egypt's great achievement and this cartoon suggests that Stalin's 'achievement' is the death of his opponents.

2

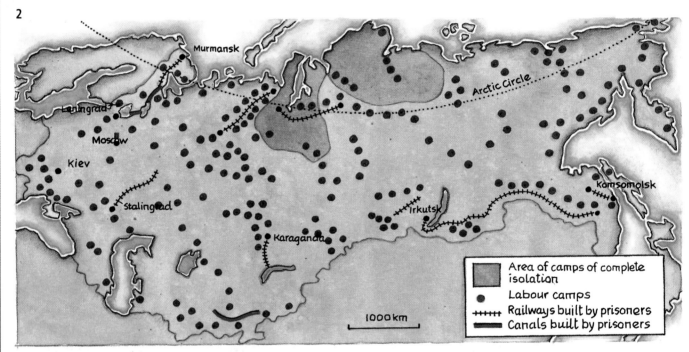

Area of camps of complete isolation
● Labour camps
╫╫╫ Railways built by prisoners
▬▬ Canals built by prisoners

1000 km

This map shows the extent of Soviet labour camps in the 1930s. Camps of complete isolation were in inhospitable areas totally cut off from other communities. In some of the northern areas the temperature could drop to as low as minus 60° C.

3 Casualties in the camps

By 1938 the death rate in prison camps was 20 per cent a year. Between 1936 and 1950, twelve million prisoners died in the camps.

4 Casualties in the army

According to Isaac Deutscher 20,000 officers, (about 25 per cent of the entire officer corps), were arrested and thousands were shot.

5 Casualties in the Party, 1935–38

'Out of 139 top Party officials, 98 were arrested and shot.'

Khrushchev in his 'Secret Speech' to the Communist Party in 1956.

6 The speed of the purges

May 1 - Marshal Tukhachevsky stands by Stalin's side to review the May Day parade.

May 12 - Tukhachevsky demoted.

June 12 - Tukhachevsky's execution announced.

QUESTIONS

1 What methods did Stalin use to control the Soviet Union?

2 List the possible reasons for Stalin's purges. Place them in order of importance and explain why you have done so.

4 Create a table like the one below. Use this and the preceding chapter to supply you with any evidence which suggests to you that Stalin was a tyrant or a genius. Write down the evidence in the chart.

TYRANT	GENIUS

3 Look at the four 'charges' directed against Stalin:

i) That he caused hardship for millions of workers and prisoners.

ii) That he caused the death of millions of peasants through collectivisation.

iii) That he murdered innocent people as 'enemies of the people'.

iv) That he developed the 'Cult of Personality'.

Your task is to consider whether or not Stalin was guilty of these 'crimes'. You need to give reasons for your answer. In a real court, guilt would have to be proved 'beyond reasonable doubt'. Your answer therefore, should be detailed evidence.

'The only purpose [of the purges] was intimidation, to plunge the whole country into a state of absolute fear, so the people not arrested would try to be perfect citizens. People carried on with their daily business, as if to say "it doesn't concern me. If what's-his-name has been arrested, there must be a good reason for it". Some people even took advantage of the terror. By reporting a neighbour to the police, they could get his flat or job.'

The poet Nadezdha Mandlestram writing about the 1930s in 'Hope Against Hope' quoted in *Stalin and Stalinism* by B. O'Callaghan.

5 How does the above source from Mandlestram help to explain how Stalin had gained almost complete control by 1941. What other evidence is there to show how much he was in control of the lives of Soviet citizens?

59

How complete was Stalin's control of the USSR?

SOURCE A

'There is much discontent and antagonism toward the government among the intelligentsia of the country and even in the Communist Party... The strength of the Stalin regime depends upon the degree to which it may rely on the army and the secret police. Voroshilov, marshal of the army, and Stalin are old "buddies". In addition, the secret police reaches down into all classes of society. It is actually an arm of Stalin's. Army and secret police serve as a check on each other; and vie with each other in loyalty to the party and to Stalin.'

'Brief of the Facts' from the US Ambassador to the Secretary of State, 6 June 1928.

SOURCE B

'In the supreme crisis of war, the ideas of the opposition, if they had been alive, might indeed have been driven to action by a conviction... that Stalin's conduct of the war was incompetent and ruinous.... His [Stalin's] reasoning probably developed along the following lines: they may want to overthrow me in a crisis — I shall charge them with having already made the attempt.'

Isaac Deutscher, in his biography of Stalin. Deutscher had been expelled from the Polish Communist Party in 1932 for his opposition to Stalin. He went to London in 1939. The first edition of his biography was published in 1949.

SOURCE C

'Freedom for several parties can exist only in a society in which there are antagonistic classes, whose interests are mutually hostile and irreconcilable.... In the USSR there is ground for only one party.'

Stalin's speech in support of the new constitution for the USSR in 1936. The new constitution brought apparent freedoms – direct and secret elections – but the one party state consolidated his hold on power.

SOURCE D

'The Great Purge was not just aimed at getting rid of Stalin's rivals, but also at welding the whole Russian nation into a machine under his control. The show trials... created an atmosphere of fear and suspicion but they united the Party under Stalin. The purges weakened the armed forces, but when Hitler invaded the Soviet Union in 1941, there was only one person the Russians could unite around – Joseph Stalin.'

P. Longworth, *Purnell's History of the 20th Century – Purges and Trials* (1969).

SOURCE E

Stalin demanded affection and few were brave enough to deny it to him. Many people were ignorant of Stalin's role in the purges and believed the propaganda levelled at the 'enemies of the state'. They felt that those in labour camps deserved their punishment.

QUESTIONS

1   What reason do these sources suggest for Stalin carrying out the purges?

2   Source C suggests the USSR was a country where there were no 'antagonistic' classes hostile to each other. Source A suggests that there was discontent and antagonism between the classes. How would you explain the differences between these two views?

3   How useful are Isaac Deutscher's comments (Source B) on Stalin? Give reasons for your answer.

4   Source E shows the love of the Soviet people for Stalin. Source D states that he created an atmosphere of fear and suspicion. Which of these sources is more reliable? Explain your answer carefully.

5   'By 1941 Stalin was in complete control of the USSR.' Is there enough evidence in these sources to prove that this opinion was correct? Give a thorough and detailed answer.

7 Review

The development of Russia and the USSR in the twentieth century was greatly influenced by three men: Nicholas II, Lenin and Stalin. Their decisions and actions directed the course of history, and different decisions could have radically altered events. Look at their profiles below and review the preceding chapters to analyse their impact on Russia and the USSR.

Nicholas Romanov. Born 1868, died 1918. Reigned 1894–1917. Son of Alexander III. Witnessed assassination of grandfather Alexander II. He was nearly assassinated himself in 1891. Fanatical believer in religious and autocratic traditions of Tsardom. No sympathy with 'senseless dreams' of political reform. Used secret police to enforce his rule and eliminate opponents. Little strength of character and little real understanding of politics. Led the Russian army in World War I despite being unsuited for high military office. Abdicated in March 1917. Murdered, along with family, by Bolsheviks in Ekaterinburg in 1918.

Vladimir Ilyich Ulyanov (Lenin). Born 1870, died 1924. Ruled Russia 1917–1924. Son of a teacher. Favourite older brother hanged in 1887 for involvement in a plot to assassinate Alexander III. Graduated in Law. Arrested in 1895 and exiled to Siberia in 1897. Left Russia in 1900 and lived in Brussels, Paris, London and Geneva. Led Bolshevik wing of Social Democratic Party. Dominant figure over the other revolutionaries, despite being in exile. Returned from Switzerland with the help of the German government. Organised successful Bolshevik takeover in November 1917. Once in power, he was forced to use terror and had to compromise some beliefs by reintroducing limited capitalism in the New Economic Policy. Weakened by assassination attempt and suffered strokes in the last two years of his life. After his death he was embalmed and kept on display in a mausoleum for the Russians to pay their respects.

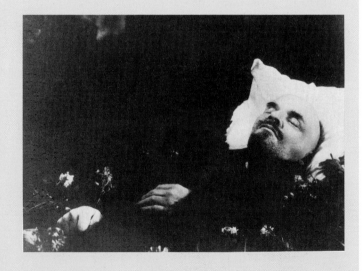

Joseph Vissarion Djugjashvili (Stalin). Born 1879, died 1953. Supreme Ruler of USSR 1929–1953. Son of a drunken, bullying shoemaker. Educated at a religious college but expelled for revolutionary views. Joined the Bolsheviks. Took part in bank raids to raise funds. Twice exiled to and escaped from Siberia. Imprisoned 1913–16. Became editor of part newspaper *Pravda* (Truth) in 1917. Became Commissar for Nationalities and General Secretary of Communist Party in Lenin's government. After Lenin's death, he promoted his own supporters and outwitted his opponents. Shared leadership up to 1928, assumed sole leadership from 1929. Imprisoned and executed possible rivals. Rapidly modernised the USSR, though at vast cost. Encouraged hero worship in a 'Cult of Personality'. Led the USSR to victory in World War II against the odds. After his death he was embalmed and placed next to Lenin. In 1956 he was denounced by his successor Khrushchev. His body was removed from the mausoleum and buried. Places named after him were renamed and across Communist Europe his statues were pulled down.

QUESTIONS

1 How do you think the background of each of these men affected their political views and methods?

2 Despite the obvious difference between them what similarities are there? Think particularly about their methods of political control.

3 An obituary details the achievements of someone and is written after their death. Write an obituary for each of these three figures looking at their achievements. Analyse how favourably or unfavourably history should judge them.

Index